BARCELONA
Like a Local

BARCELONA
Like a Local

BY THE PEOPLE WHO CALL IT HOME

Contents

NIGHTLIFE

OUTDOORS

meet the locals

HARRI DAVIES

Writer Harri left Britain for Barna for a year, and ended up staying for five. They're happiest when dancing the night away and taking a dip in the sea.

TERESA GOTTEIN MARTÍNEZ

Austrian-born journalist Teresa was seven when she moved to Spain. Living between London and Barna, she loves meeting her pals in Gràcia.

THOM LAMPON-MASTERS

Thom moved to the city ten years ago to learn the lingo. He spends his days stumbling between dive bars and bookshops, all while making the most of his linguistic skills as a translator.

SOFÍA ROBLEDO

When writer and Barcelona native Sofía isn't scribbling away in the library (her favourite place), she's hiking in the Collserola hills.

SAM ZUCKER

American travel writer, photographer and pro chef Sam enjoys exploring the city with his young daughter. Oh, and inline skating, his new hobby.

Barcelona
WELCOME TO THE CITY

Barcelona has long been a rebel. Here artists and architects break new ground, writers pen pointed literature and queer artists perform loudly and proudly. Perhaps most famously, though, Barcelona has often taken centre stage in the fight for Catalan independence. Though tides may be changing to some extent, you're still far more likely to see the Catalan flag hanging from someone's balcony than you will the Spanish.

Yes, Barna (take note: Barça is the football club) is a complex city. It's a place of bubbling tension and fierce unity; a paradox of beauty and grime, tradition and modernity. And it's these wonderful contradictions that make Barcelonans so incredibly proud of their beloved city. And why shouldn't they be? Just look around. LGBTQ+ bars sit next door to Gothic churches, cycle lanes wind around *Modernista* mansions, vintage markets pop up in old factories and ultra-modern art galleries stand in medieval palaces.

No wonder, then, that Barcelonans get annoyed by *guiris* (a scathing name for tourists) who think Barna is just sea, sand and sangria. And that's exactly why you need this book – to show you what really makes Barcelona the fierce and fabled city that it is. We'll show you the vermouth bars where locals have been mingling for decades, the nightclubs that are definitely worth staying up late for (we really do mean late) and the very best spots to *tapear* (go for tapas). Of course, we can't capture every local's version of Barcelona, but we can offer a taste of the city's infectious spirit.

So, whether you're a visitor looking to go beyond the stereotypes, or a local in need of fresh inspiration, this book is here to help. Don't be a *guiri* – visit Barcelona the local way.

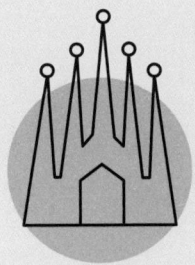

Liked by the locals

"If you try to describe Barcelona, your words will change like a kaleidoscope: one second, the city is a cosmopolitan metropolis, the next moment, it's steeped in traditions. That's what I love most about it – there's always a different side to unearth."

THOM LAMPON-MASTERS,
WRITER AND TRANSLATOR

Hedonistic festivals in summer, age-old traditions in autumn and merry-making fun in winter: there's always something afoot in this transgressive city.

Barcelona
THROUGH THE YEAR

SPRING

TIME ON THE TERRACES
As the weather starts to warm up, crowds flood back to Barna's plentiful outdoor terraces to while away afternoons with friends.

SANT JORDI
On 23 April, the day of Catalonia's patron saint (Sant Jordi, or St George), booksellers take over the city streets and locals exchange roses and books with their loved ones.

NIGHT AT THE MUSEUM
A free dose of culture tempts Barcelonans on International Museums Day in May, with institutions staying open late into the night.

SUMMER

FESTES MAJORS
Locals love a summertime street party. Every *barri* has its own but Festes de Gràcia draws the biggest crowds of Barcelonans thanks to its incredible handmade street decorations.

SUMMER SWIMS
In summer, the days are hot and the nights are long. So, after a hard day's work, friends and families make their way to the beach for a refreshing dip and sundowner or two.

FESTIVAL FUN
Barcelona stages more music festivals than any one person's wallet (or liver) could possibly cope with. Throngs of

revellers dance the night away at the likes of Primavera Sound, Sónar, Vida and Cruïlla – to name but a few.

THE AUGUST ADÉU
Barna reaches melting point in August. Businesses work shorter hours, or shut altogether, and locals flee the sweltering city to travel or visit family in cooler climes.

AUTUMN

FALL FORAGING
As the nights draw in, friends spend their Saturdays hiking in the mountains, looking out for mushrooms, before heading home to cook up a feast.

LA MERCÈ
Barcelonans can't get enough of September's La Mercè, the city's annual festival. It's a week of *castells* (human towers), *gegants* (giant parading figures) and the traditional *correfoc* (fire run).

LA CASTANYADA
Nothing says autumn in Barna like the smell of chestnuts roasting over hot coals. On 31 October, locals eat *panellets* (marzipan cakes coated in nuts) washed down with sweet wine.

This tradition dates back centuries, when bell-ringers would eat chestnuts while pealing for the dead.

WINTER

COSY CAFÉ VISITS
As things cool off, Barcelonans gravitate toward the city's *xocolateries* for warming mugs of thick, gloopy hot chocolate.

CHRISTMAS IN THE CITY
December is a blur of work lunches and nights out with pals before the main event: Christmas Day. Catalans get together with family to beat their *Tió de Nadal* (a smiling log) with sticks until it secretes presents. We kid you not.

HAVE A GRAPE YEAR
Come midnight, locals welcome the new year by stuffing a grape into their mouth with each strike of the clock.

CARNIVAL
While many Catholic traditions have fallen out of practice in Catalunya, some have stuck around. Carnival's week-long festivities include parades, fancy dress competitions and sardine burials, while Sitges *(p183)* hosts party-oriented events.

There's an art to being a Barcelonan, from the dos and don'ts on the beach to negotiating the city's streets. Here's a breakdown of all you need to know.

Barcelona
KNOW-HOW

For a directory of health and safety resources, safe spaces and accessibility information, turn to page 186. For everything else, read on.

EAT
Except for breakfast, which is munched on the hoof, eating is a social affair and never rushed in Barcelona. Lunch is the main meal of the day and eaten from 2pm, followed by a siesta. Dinners are lighter and kick off any time after 8pm. At the weekend, an aperitif is a must, as is the beloved post-dinner *sobretaula* – the tradition of chatting around the table, coffees and digestifs in hand.

DRINK
Pavement bars and cafés are second living rooms for Barcelonans, who often head down to their local to read the paper with a coffee or catch-up with a friend. If you're sitting outside, the staff will come out to take your order; if you're inside, you'll generally be expected to order at the counter. These laid-back spots close around midnight, or an hour later on weekends.

SHOP
All the usual suspects (hello Zara) line the city's main shopping streets but locals prefer to shop in the city's indie stores and markets (where haggling is a no-no). Wherever you're spending your hard-earned cash, it's always worth carrying a tote bag to avoid the charge for a plastic one.

Shops open at 9am and close at 8 or 9pm, with smaller businesses shutting their doors between 2 and 4pm for lunch. On Sundays, pretty much everything closes for at least the afternoon, if not the whole day.

ARTS & CULTURE

Culture comes at a price in Barcelona, with many museums charging €10–13. The good news is a lot of places are free to enter at least one afternoon a week or month – check museum websites for details. Theatre, spoken word and comedy is largely performed in Catalan or Spanish. Fancy a gig instead? Barcelonans love live music, so it's wise to book any and all concerts in advance to avoid disappointment.

NIGHTLIFE

A chilled night out in Barna involves a few drinks with friends at a pavement bar or terrace. Those looking to go big, meanwhile, start with "pre-drinks" at home before hitting the clubs any time after 2am (an afternoon siesta is a must). Dancing continues until 5 or 6am, when the clubs shut, so many welcome the morning with a final drink at a dive bar or on the beach at sunrise. There's no need to dress up, but beachwear and flip-flops will attract some eye-rolls.

OUTDOORS

Barcelonans are an outdoorsy bunch, whiling away their days in the park or on the beach. Off to join them on the sand? Keep a close eye on your belongings as pickpocketing is a problem. As for rubbish, there's loads of recycling bins across the city so be sure to do your bit (*guiris*, aka tourists, are known for being litterbugs, a reputation we want to help stamp out). Oh, and don't forget sunscreen.

Keep in mind

Here are some more tips and tidbits that will help you fit in like a local.

» **Cash vs card** The majority of places accept contactless payments but it's always worth keeping some cash on you.

» **No smoking** There's a ban on smoking inside and on a handful of city beaches. If you do need to light up, make sure to throw the cigarette butt in a bin.

» **Tipping** It's always a nice gesture to tip waiters a few euros, but it's not obligatory.

» **Stay hydrated** Barna is home to countless free drinking fountains, so bring a resuable bottle to fill up on your travels.

GETTING AROUND

Catalunya's capital is divided into a handful of *barris*, or neighbourhoods *(p14)*, where some 1.6 million people live. Most of Barcelona is organized on a grid system, particularly the neighbourhoods of Eixample and Poblenou; with the Collserola mountains behind them and the gridded streets sloping down to the sea beyond, it's easy to get your bearings around these parts. The older winding streets of the Gothic Quarter and Raval are more confusing. Just remember: Las Ramblas runs straight between them from Plaça de Catalunya to the water's edge.

To help you out, we've provided what3words addresses for each sight in this book, meaning you can quickly pinpoint exactly where you're heading.

On foot

Barcelona is not a big city, so it's easy to get around on foot. Some steeper *barris* even have escalators to take the edge off. And, on weekends, the council closes off some of the main streets to traffic, allowing pedestrians more space and less fumes. Nice, eh? Of course, walking in the heat can be tiring. Be sure to have plenty of water and check out the Cool Walks website to plan your route through the city's most shaded streets.

Life in Barcelona is more slow-paced than in other European cities, so you won't have locals hot on your heels. That said, if you need to stop and check your phone or take a photo, step aside to let them sidle past.

https://cool.bcnregional.com

On wheels

Barcelonans love pedal power, with many locals choosing to cycle to work. Bike lanes generally follow the city's one-way system. The traffic light system also applies to bikes, so never go through a red light (even if you see fellow cyclists doing it). Cycling on the pavement when you could be in a bike lane will be met by shouts, and cycling with headphones is illegal – the police are strict about this. It's also illegal to cycle over the limit (0.5mg of alcohol per litre of blood, which works out as a pint of beer). Finally, always wear a helmet. No excuses.

The council's bike sharing scheme, Bicing, is only available for residents. Good news: Donkey Republic provides bikes that anyone can pick up and drop off around the city using its app. It's €1 for a 15-minute pedal, €5 for six hours or €12 for a full day. A lot of locals prefer to nip around the city on mopeds. For those who don't own their own, sharing

schemes from eCooltra and Yego are on hand to rent mopeds by the hour or day.
www.donkey.bike
www.cooltra.com
www.rideyego.com

By public transport

Barcelona's transport network, which is run by TMB, includes the metro, bus and tram. The metro runs from 5am to midnight on weekdays and until 2am on weekends (this is Barcelona, after all). While the metro map is easy enough to use, the bus map can seem daunting. Just remember: the H lines run horizontally, the V lines run vertically and the D lines diagonally. You've got this.

Download and register with TMB's app and use your smartphone as a contactless ticket. Prefer a paper ticket? Buy a "T-Casual" ticket for €12.15 and get ten trips across the network.

By car and taxi

Parking in Barna is no easy feat. This is largely intentional; the council is transforming traffic lanes into pavement space and bike lanes, much to the approval of eco-conscious locals. While many aren't, therefore, investing in cars, they are still taking taxis and ride-sharing services like Cabify (no Uber here), especially after a night out.

Download these

We recommend you download these apps to help you get about the city.

WHAT3WORDS

Your geocoding friend

A what3words address is a simple way to communicate any precise location on earth, using just three words. ///divides.sharp.desktop, for example, is the code for the entrance to the Gaudí House Museum. Simply download the free what3words app, type a what3words address into the search bar, and you'll know exactly where to go.

TMBAPP

Your local transit advice

The app from TMB, the Barcelona transport service, helps you plan your journey, find your nearest bus stop or station, check for operating hours and delays, and use your smartphone as a contactless ticket.

Each and every **barri** *(neighbourhood) in Barna has its own history and culture – and is very proud of the fact. Here we take a look at some of our favourites.*

Barcelona
NEIGHBOURHOODS

Barceloneta

Glitzy hotels and an artificial beach might tempt the tourists but this district also offers old-school bodegas and traditional street parties. Once a fishing neighbourhood, Barceloneta became a refuge for families forced out of Born due to the construction of Parc de la Ciutadella in the 1800s. It's no wonder, then, that the *barri's* locals actively protest against gentrification in their patch today. *{map 5}*

Born

Technically called "Sant Pere, Santa Catalina i la Ribera", Born is a labyrinth of medieval streets. Locals expertly navigate these alleyways, ducking into the *barri's* artisan stores and workshops, just as locals did centuries ago. *{map 1}*

Eixample

Vast and gridded Eixample buzzes with life, day and night. Through the *barri's* heart runs Passeig de Gràcia, a grand old street lined with *Modernista* mansions, high-end stores and swanky restaurants. Either side of this thoroughfare is where middle-class families go about their days, picking the kids up from school and swinging by their local library. Around the quadrants of Universitat, LGBTQ+ folk and their allies live their best lives in "Gaixample"'s rip-roaring bars. *{map 4}*

Gothic Quarter

Neighbourhoods don't come more historical than this place. Roman ruins, ancient streets and a medieval Jewish quarter attract throngs of wide-eyed tourists. As for the locals? They prefer the Gothic Quarter's shabby-chic bars, hidden down the streets toward the sea. *{map 1}*

Gràcia

Once a town on the outskirts of the city, Gràcia is nirvana for young families who can't get enough of the bohemian *barri's* organic shops, vermouth bars and vegan cafés. Locals live life publicly here, spending lazy mornings and sociable afternoons in the pavement cafés that circle the neighbourhood's squares. *{map 4}*

Montjuïc

Ah, Montjuïc: the stunning setting of the 1992 Olympic Games. Sure, it's more of a string of parks than a traditional neighbourhood, but Barna's Magic Mountain teems with life nonetheless. Families hold outdoor celebrations in its green spaces, folks enjoy a dose of culture at its world-class museums and wannabe Olympians make use of the running tracks. *{map 3}*

Poblenou

The former hub of Barcelona's industry is now the heartland of young coffee-clutching professionals. Old factories house artists' studios and cultural centres, plus the tech sector "Districte 22". Barcelona's version of Silicon Valley, this urban renewal project is aimed at tech start-ups. *{map 5}*

Poble Sec

Multicultural and working-class Poble Sec has managed to keep its edge in a city that's fast-gentrifying. The little *barri*, at the foot of Montjuïc, is hard to beat for top-quality tapas joints, cheap and cheerful dive bars, and lively nightclubs. *{map 3}*

Raval

Mischief has long been the hallmark of this notorious part of town. Once a hot bed of crime and sex work, the *barri* has since seen an influx of immigration, with families from Latin America, the Philippines and Pakistan settling here. Kebab shops and falafel stands buzz with energy in the evening, when good-timers stop to refuel on wild nights out in the city's most rebellious neighbourhood. *{map 2}*

Sant Antoni

Hot on Gràcia's heels as a hipster's paradise is Sant Antoni. The uber-cool *barri* is awash with bougie brunch spots and trendy clothing stores, plus old-school Catalan restaurants and charming *orxateries*. *{map 3}*

Sants

A working-class district to its core, Sants stands firm as the final frontier against gentrification. Cultural associations, workers' cooperatives and traditional businesses form the social fabric of this residential outpost. *{map 6}*

Sarrià

The upper parts of the city (in and around the rolling Collserola hills) are also home to its upper classes. Sarrià is one such posh patch. Expect beautiful townhouses, expensive wine bars and fancy gourmet shops galore. *{map 6}*

Tibidabo and Vallvidrera

Only rich folk – those even richer than Sarrià residents – can afford to live in these leafy neighbourhoods, set up high in the Collserola hills. For those who can only dream, the surroundings are perfect for gusty weekend hikes and scenic bike rides. *{map 6}*

Barcelona
ON THE MAP

Whether you're looking for your new favourite spot or want to check out what each part of Barcelona has to offer, our maps – along with handy map references throughout the book – have you covered.

Parc de Collserola

TIBIDABO

RONDA DE DALT

SARRIÀ

AVINGUDA

CARRER   DE

SANT FELIU DE LLOBREGAT

B23

A2

B23

ESPLUGUES DE LLOBREGAT

CORNELLÀ DE LLOBREGAT

L'HOSPITALET DE LLOBREGAT

A2

El Llobregat

SANT BOI DE LLOBREGAT

C31

BADALONA

SANTA COLOMA DE GRAMENET

SANT ADRIÀ DE BESÒS

SANT ANDREU DE PALOMAR

HORTA

SANT MARTÍ

VALLCARCA

AVINGUDA MERIDIANA

RONDA DE DALT

RONDA LITORAL

GRAN VIA DE LES CORTS CATALANES

AVINGUDA DIAGONAL

C33

B20

C31

4

GRÀCIA

5

POBLENOU

EIXAMPLE

CATALANES

DIAGONAL

3

2

1

GOTHIC QUARTER

LES CORTS

RAVAL

SANTS

SANTS

GRAN VIA DE

BARCELONETA

MONTJUÏC

B10

Mediterranean Sea

0 kilometres   2

0 miles   2

PLAÇA D'URQUINAONA

C. DE TRAFALGAR

VIA LAIETANA

SANT PERE

CARRER DEL COMERÇ

Plaça de Sant Agustí Vell D

A Palau de la Música Catalana

Mescladís del Pou N

C. DE SANT PERE MES BAIX

Antic Teatre N
E Le Cucine Mandarosso

S Humana Vintage

S Raima

CARRER COMTAL

AV. DE FRANCESC CAMBO

Mercat de Santa Caterina

CARRER DE LA PRINCESA

D Planelles Donat

La Casa del Entremesos A

CARRER DELS CARDERS

E Bar del Pla

AV. DEL PORTAL DE L'ANGEL

A Els Quatre Gats

A MuchaFibra

PLAÇA D'ANTONI MAURA

Marlowe Bar D

Museu Picasso A

BORN

VIA LAIETANA

Can Cisa D

Moco Museum D

La Chinata A

PASSEIG DEL BORN

PLAÇA NOVA

GOTHIC QUARTER

Bodega la Puntual D

A Taller de 4 Pintors

CARRER DE LA PORTAFERISSA

PLAÇA DE L'ANGEL

Dr Stravinsky D

S Angle Store

E Estimar

Xocolates Fargas S

CARRER DE LA PALLA

CARRER DEL BISBE

Bon Vent S

E El Chigre 1769

O Plaça de Sant Felip Neri

Cafés el Magnífico D

La Botifarreria de Santa Maria

Conesa E

CARRER DE JAUME I

L'Arca S

E La Alcoba Azul

D Zona d'Ombra

S Casa Carot

Dulcinea D

MUHBA El Call

VIA LAIETANA

S O Plaça del Pi

A

Collage D S

Vila Viniteca "La Teca"

Ganiveteria Roca

PLAÇA DE SANT JAUME

CARRER DE LA CIUTAT

A The Espadrilles Experience

PLAÇA DELS TRAGINERS

PLAÇA D'ANTONI LOPEZ

CARRER DE LA BOQUERIA

CARRER DE FERRAN

CARRER D'AVINYO

CARRER AMPLE

PLAÇA DE LA BOQUERIA

Can Culleretes E

PORT VELL

LA RAMBLA

Manchester N

CARRER DE SANT PAU

PLAÇA REIAL

Marula Café N

PASSEIG DE COLOM

Jamboree Jazz S

N Ocaña

Macarena Club N

Polaroid Bar N

PLAÇA DE LA MERCE

MOLL DE LA FUSTA

0 metres 250
0 yards 250

LA RAMBLA

PLAÇA DEL DUC DE MEDINACELI

MAP 1

ⓔ EAT

Bar del Pla *(p48)*
Bodega la Puntual *(p51)*
Can Culleretes *(p33)*
Conesa *(p46)*
El Chigre 1769 *(p39)*
Estimar *(p55)*
La Alcoba Azul *(p49)*
Le Cucine Mandarosso *(p52)*
San Pedrito *(p52)*

ⓓ DRINK

Bar Paradiso *(p79)*
Cafés el Magnífico *(p69)*
Can Cisa *(p67)*
Collage *(p78)*
Dr Stravinsky *(p78)*
Dulcinea *(p80)*
Marlowe Bar *(p76)*
Planelles Donat *(p82)*
Zona d'Ombra *(p65)*

ⓢ SHOP

Angle Store *(p104)*
Bon Vent *(p96)*
Casa Carot *(p111)*
Ganiveteria Roca *(p99)*
Humana Vintage *(p88)*
La Botifarreria de Santa Maria *(p110)*
La Chinata *(p110)*
L'Arca *(p89)*
Mercat de Santa Caterina *(p109)*

Raima *(p96)*
Vila Viniteca "La Teca" *(p108)*
Xocolates Fargas *(p110)*

ⓐ ARTS & CULTURE

El Born Centre de Cultura i Memòria *(p118)*
Els Quatre Gats *(p120)*
The Espadrilles Experience *(p134)*
La Casa del Entremesos *(p128)*
Moco Museum *(p126)*
MuchaFibra *(p134)*
MUHBA El Call *(p118)*
Museu Picasso *(p124)*
Palau de la Música Catalana *(p121)*
Taller de 4 Pintors *(p133)*

ⓝ NIGHTLIFE

Antic Teatre *(p156)*
Guzzo Club *(p150)*
Jamboree Jazz *(p155)*
Macarena Club *(p147)*
Manchester *(p151)*
Marula Café *(p146)*
Mescladís del Pou *(p158)*
Ocaña *(p149)*
Polaroid Bar *(p150)*

ⓞ OUTDOORS

Plaça del Pi *(p171)*
Plaça de Sant Augustí Vell *(p171)*
Plaça de Sant Felip Neri *(p170)*

MAP 2

EIXAMPLE

Morro Fi

CARRER DEL

CARRER D'ARAGÓ

Bar Alegría

COMTE BORRELL

Vermuteria
La Lola

SANT
ANTONI

RAVAL

PLAÇA DELS
ANGELS

RAMBLA DEL RAVAL

RONDA DE SANT ANTONI

CARRER DE LES CORTS CATALANES

Cinc Sentits
Cruix

Safari
Disco Club

Parc
Joan Miró

CARRER DE SEPULVEDA

Can Vilaró

Els Sortidors
del Parlament
Sirvent
Superilla Parlament/Borrell

Marcapáginas

Conservas
Latorre

Federal Café

GRAN VIA DE LES CORTS CATALANES

AVINGUDA DE MISTRAL

Bar Calders

Brava
Fabrics

Centre LGBTI

PLAÇA
D'ESPANYA

AVINGUDA DEL PARAL·LEL

AVINGUDA DEL PARAL·LEL

PLAÇA DE
LAS NAVAS

La Federica

POBLE SEC

Esparteria
Lluch

PLAÇA DE
L'UNIVERS

CARRER DE LLEIDA

Espai
Salvadiscos

C. DE LA CONCORDIA

Celler
Cal Marino

CARRER NOU DE LA RAMBLA

Bodega
Amposta

CaixaForum

AVINGUDA DE RIUS I TAULET

Taberna Noroeste

La Raposa
C. DE MAGALHAES

PLAÇA DE
JOSEP PUIG
I CADAFALCH

Jardins de Laribal
& Teatre Grec

Piscina
Municipal Salts
Montjuïc

Upload

La Terrrazza

MNAC

Fundació
Joan Miró

AVINGUDA DE MIRAMAR

Jardins de
Mossèn Cinto
Verdaguer

PLAÇA DEL
MIRADOR

Jardí Botànic
Històric

AVINGUDA DE L'ESTADI

Jardins de
Joan Maragall

Museum of the Olympics
& Sport and Olympic Stadium

AVINGUDA DEL CASTELL

MONTJUÏC

Estadi
Olímpic

Jardí Petra
Kelly

Anella Olímpica

Castell de
Montjuïc

PASSEIG OLÍMPIC

Jardí
Botànic

PASSEIG DEL MIGDIA

0 metres   500
0 yards   500

MAP 3

E EAT

Bar Alegría *(p48)*
Bodega Amposta *(p51)*
Can Vilaró *(p34)*
Cinc Sentits *(p54)*
Conservas Latorre *(p47)*
Cruix *(p36)*
Taberna Noroeste *(p39)*
Terraza Martínez *(p54)*

D DRINK

Celler Cal Marino *(p67)*
Els Sortidors del Parlament *(p67)*
Federal Café *(p69)*
Morro Fi *(p60)*
Sirvent *(p80)*
Vermuteria La Lola *(p63)*

S SHOP

Brava Fabrics *(p105)*
Espai Salvadiscos *(p102)*
Esparteria Lluch *(p97)*
La Raposa *(p93)*
Marcapáginas *(p94)*

A ARTS & CULTURE

CaixaForum *(p127)*
Castell de Montjuïc *(p117)*
Centre LGBTI *(p130)*

Fundació Joan Miró *(p127)*
MNAC *(p125)*
Museum of the Olympics & Sport and Olympic Stadium *(p119)*

N NIGHTLIFE

Apolo *(p144)*
Bar Calders *(p157)*
La Federica *(p142)*
La Terrrazza *(p146)*
Laut *(p147)*
Safari Disco Club *(p140)*
Sala Upload *(p145)*
Salts *(p159)*

O OUTDOORS

Anella Olímpica *(p178)*
Jardí Botànic Històric *(p177)*
Jardins de Joan Maragall *(p178)*
Jardins de Laribal & Teatre Grec *(p177)*
Jardins de Mossèn Costa i Llobera *(p178))*
Piscina Municipal Montjuïc *(p175)*
Superilla Parlament/Borrell *(p168)*

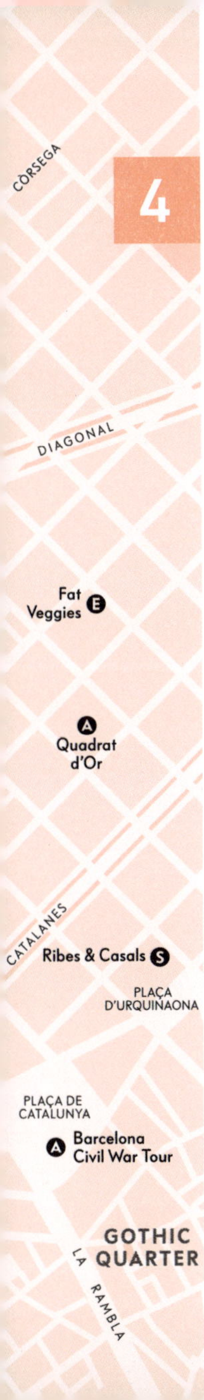

E EAT

Berbena *(p38)*
Besta *(p38)*
Cal Boter *(p32)*
Fat Veggies *(p43)*
La Bikineria *(p46)*
La Ceba *(p35)*
Mont Bar *(p37)*
Rabipelao *(p40)*
Ramen-Ya Hiro *(p44)*
Robata *(p54)*
Silan *(p55)*
Veg World India *(p40)*

D DRINK

Bar Bodega Quimet *(p66)*
Bar La Camila *(p68)*
Bar Raïm *(p74)*
Bar Salvatge *(p64)*
Bodega Marin *(p60)*
Las Vermudas *(p61)*
La Vermu *(p63)*
Senyor Vermut *(p61)*
SlowMov *(p68)*
Syra *(p71)*
Xocolateria La Nena *(p82)*

S SHOP

Altaïr *(p92)*
Cotton Vintage *(p88)*
El Genio Equivocado *(p103)*
Entre Latas *(p111)*
Finestres *(p95)*
Hibernian *(p95)*
Jazz Messengers *(p102)*
La Central *(p93)*
Odd Kiosk *(p95)*
Ribes & Casals *(p98)*

A ARTS & CULTURE

Art&Wine *(p132)*
Atuell Ceràmica *(p134)*
Barcelona Civil War Tour *(p116)*
Casa Amatller *(p123)*
Fundació Tàpies *(p126)*
Quadrat d'Or *(p120)*

N NIGHTLIFE

Believe Club *(p142)*
Candy Darling *(p141)*
Carita Bonita *(p141)*
Curtis Audiophile Café *(p150)*
Heliogàbal *(p153)*
La Chapelle *(p140)*

O OUTDOORS

Plaça de la Vila de Gràcia *(p170)*
Plaça del Sol *(p170)*

MAP 5

5

Skatepark
Mar Bella
◉
*Platja de
la Mar Bella*
◉
Barcelona
Beach House

*Platja del
Bogatell*

🅔 EAT

Bar Jai-Ca *(p49)*
Bodega Bonay *(p36)*
Cheriff *(p53)*
Compá *(p47)*
Flax & Kale *(p41)*
Funky Bakers Deli *(p45)*
Roots & Rolls *(p43)*

🅓 DRINK

Balius *(p76)*
Bar Leo *(p72)*
Bodega Maestrazgo *(p66)*
El Tío Che *(p82)*
News & Coffee *(p70)*
Nomad Coffee Lab *(p71)*

🆂 SHOP

Barcelona City Records *(p100)*
BLAW Store *(p105)*
Fantastik *(p99)*
Mercat dels Encants *(p90)*
Petits Encants *(p89)*
Pitagora *(p107)*
SSSTUFFF *(p107)*
Ultra-Local Records *(p101)*

🅐 ARTS & CULTURE

Biblioteca Pública Arús *(p131)*
Disseny Hub *(p125)*
IDEAL *(p128)*
Kanay Taller de Ceràmica *(p132)*

🅝 NIGHTLIFE

Càmping *(p157)*
L'Auditori *(p152)*
La Monroe *(p159)*
Razzmatazz *(p144)*
Terrassa de les Indianes *(p158)*
Vol *(p152)*

🅞 OUTDOORS

Barcelona Beach House *(p173)*
Espigó del Gas *(p172)*
Inercia Rollerblade Rental *(p172)*
Parc de la Ciutadella *(p176)*
Plaça de la Rosa dels Vents *(p168)*
Skatepark Mar Bella *(p175)*
Ungravity SUP & Surf *(p175)*

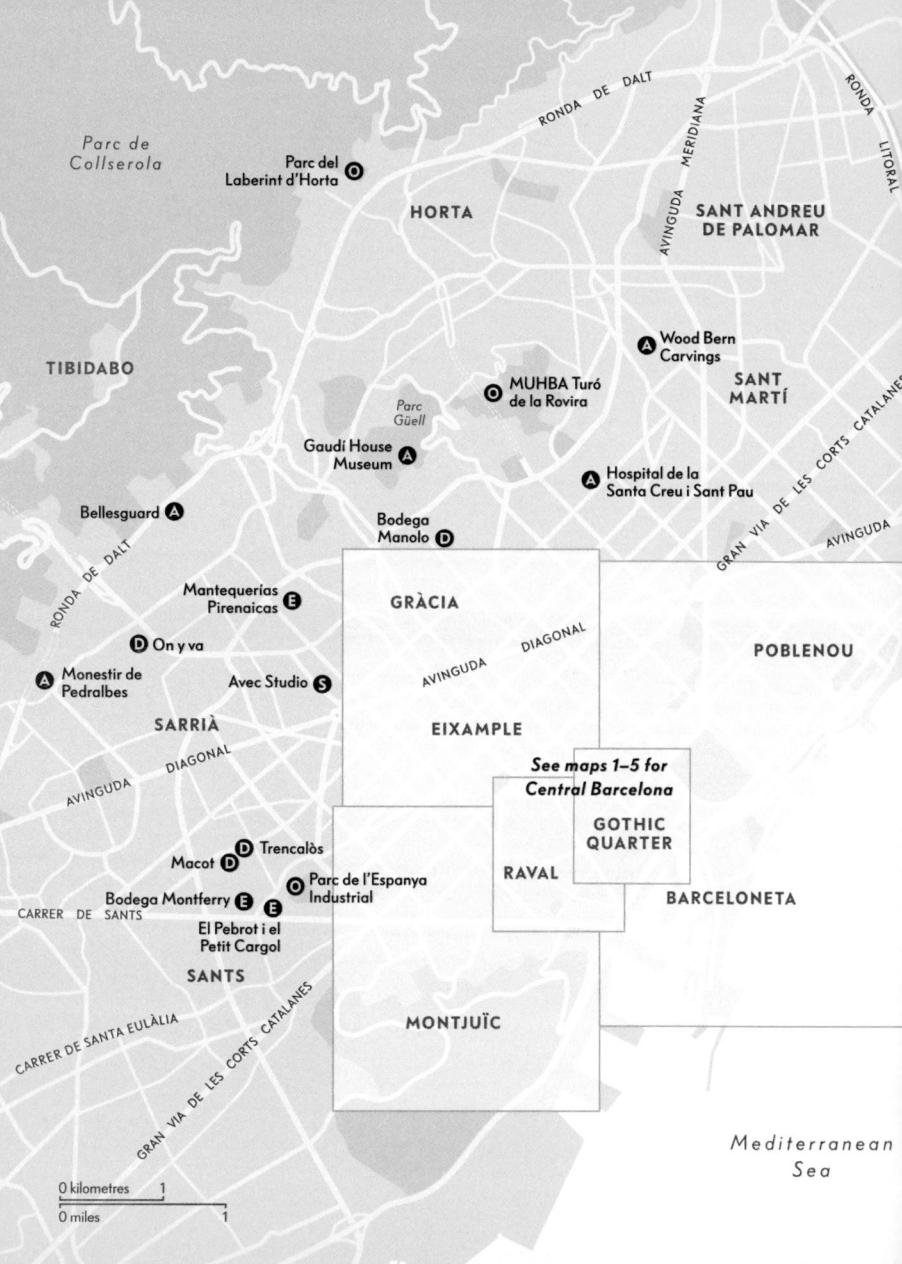

Parc de
Collserola

Parc del
Laberint d'Horta Ⓞ

HORTA

RONDA DE DALT

AVINGUDA MERIDIANA

RONDA LITORAL

SANT ANDREU
DE PALOMAR

TIBIDABO

Wood Bern
Ⓐ Carvings

SANT
MARTÍ

MUHBA Turó
Ⓞ de la Rovira

Parc
Güell

GRAN VIA DE LES CORTS CATALANES

Gaudí House
Museum Ⓐ

Ⓐ Hospital de la
Santa Creu i Sant Pau

AVINGUDA

Bellesguard Ⓐ

RONDA DE DALT

Bodega
Manolo Ⓓ

POBLENOU

Mantequerías
Pirenaicas Ⓔ

GRÀCIA

Ⓓ On y va

AVINGUDA   DIAGONAL

Monestir de
Ⓐ Pedralbes

Avec Studio Ⓢ

SARRIÀ

EIXAMPLE

See maps 1–5 for
Central Barcelona

DIAGONAL

AVINGUDA

GOTHIC
QUARTER

BARCELONETA

RAVAL

Macot Ⓓ

Ⓓ Trencalòs

Bodega Montferry Ⓔ

Ⓔ

Ⓞ Parc de l'Espanya
Industrial

CARRER DE SANTS

El Pebrot i el
Petit Cargol

SANTS

MONTJUÏC

CARRER DE SANTA EULÀLIA

GRAN VIA DE LES CORTS CATALANES

Mediterranean
Sea

0 kilometres   1

0 miles   1

MAP 6

EAT

Feasts whipped up by families, plates of tasty tapas passed between loved ones, creative dishes crafted by plucky chefs: eating out in Barna is all about celebrating life.

Traditional Fare

Catalans are fiercely – and rightly – proud of their cuisine. Barcelona has loads of traditional (read: old-school) spots plating up classic Catalan and Spanish dishes. Here is a taster to whet your appetite.

CAL BOTER

Map 4; Carrer de Tordera 62, Gràcia; ///juniors.burns.shorten; www.restaurantcalboter.com

Brunch culture may be synonymous with gentrification and touristification, but Barcelonans are fighting back by indulging in their own traditional mid-morning meal: *esmorzars de forquilla* (literally "fork breakfasts"). Coined by essayist Josep Pla back in the 1950s, the term refers to the local tradition of an early feast

Try it!
COOK LIKE A CATALAN

Looking to learn from the masters? Born to Cook offers various gourmet experiences. Better yet, the class leaders will help you navigate Barcelona's vast Santa Caterina market *(www.borntocookbarcelona.com)*.

of hearty dishes and tortillas. Forget brunch mimosas: at Cal Boter, you can raise a glass of wine poured from a traditional *porró* jug and start your day the Catalan way.

L'ESTUPENDU

Map 6; Carrer d'Eduard Maristany, 75, Badalona;
///scooped.jumped.bake; www.grupovarela.es/l-estupendu
Step in past the palm trees and blue picket fence and take a seat under the shade of the straw roof at L'Estupendu. Being by the seafront, seafood is, of course, king at this beach restaurant, so a paella-style rice dish is a lunchtime must, and the perfect thing to share with friends while gazing out to sea.

>> **Don't leave without** sharing an *arròs del fadrí*, a seafood rice dish in which all the seafood comes mercifully ready peeled.

CAN CULLERETES

Map 1; Carrer d'en Quintana, 5, Gothic Quarter;
///exacted.beeline.sizes; www.culleretes.com
With wrought-iron chandeliers and elaborate wall tapestries, Can Culleretes oozes all the character you'd expect to find in Catalunya's oldest restaurant (it was founded way back when in 1796). The menu likewise has all the essential pickings of Catalan cuisine: meatballs with cuttlefish, stuffed aubergines, *botifarra* sausages. But don't go thinking all that history and top-notch grub comes with a hefty price tag; the set lunch menu is a steal. *Bon profit!* (That's *bon appétit* in Catalan.)

EL PEBROT I EL PETIT CARGOL

Map 6; Carrer d'Alcolea 18, Sants; ///wedding.nagging.steep;
934 316 870

If the "you come here to suck and enjoy" sign wasn't enough of a giveaway, then the snail logo outside this tiny shop makes its speciality clear: yep, tasty snails. Tuck into this Catalan dish the traditional way, served up in a range of tasty sauces. Not for you? There are plenty of snail-free options, too.

NA MINDONA

Map 2; Carrer de la Riereta 8, Raval; ///terminology.burst.spending;
www.namindona.es

You could easily walk past Na Mindona were it not for the vase of flowers that Xisca – one of the friendliest restaurateurs in town – sets outside every day. Watch her flit between tables and chat to her guests like old friends, talking them through her Majorcan menu. Our favourite dish? It's between the fishy rice stew and tongue with capers.

» Don't leave without finishing with a digestif of the traditional Majorcan *licor d'herbes. Salut!*

CAN VILARÓ

Map 3; Carrer del Comte Borrell, 61, Sant Antoni;
///matter.promises.palace; 933 250 578

For three generations the Vilaró family have been keeping the working people of Sant Antoni well fed. Even while much of the *barri* (neighbourhood) has gentrified and succumbed to food fads, the Vilaró family has stayed true to traditional Catalan cuisine in its meatiest forms (pig trotters, lamb lungs and blood sausage all feature heavily on the menu). Rest easy: there are dishes for the more faint-hearted, but when in Barcelona...

LA CEBA

Map 4; Carrer de la Perla, 10, Gràcia; ///hills.overnight.elastic; www.lacebabcn.com

Anyone familiar with Spanish cuisine will be aware of the humble *tortilla de patatas* (a traditional Spanish omelette bulked out with potatoes). La Ceba takes this classic dish to a whole new level with some 50 types of omelette, each served with a slice of mouth-wateringly good tomato-drenched toast (a Catalan staple). It's these endless varieties of omelettes – and the good-value set-menu lunches – that keep Gràcia locals coming back.

Shh!

Yes, Les Ramblas is a tourist trap. But behind the souvenir stores and pricey pavement cafés hides the odd treasure, like Louro *(Rambla dels Caputxins, 37)*. Few seem to have cottoned on to the fact that this charming Galician restaurant is tucked away on the first floor of an old palace. Enter under the Hostal Benidorm sign and climb the stairs up to Louro, where couples chow down on Galician-style octopus and smugly toast to their choice of restaurant.

Creative Cuisine

Classic fare will always have its place but Barcelona is also a city of innovation and reinvention. Not all these creative spots are uber-fancy, but all of them promise unadulterated deliciousness.

BODEGA BONAY

Map 5; Gran Via de les Corts Catalanes, 700, Eixample;
///luck.robots.ensemble; www.casabonay.com

Found within the hip Casa Bonay hotel, Bodega Bonay curates small plates of mostly Catalan influence, with seasonal ingredients. Our top tip? Come here in winter. The stuff they do with sea urchins is magic, and the artichoke tart tatin (complete with a crispy filo base) is the ultimate comfort food. Round off your meal at the rooftop bar.

CRUIX

Map 3; Carrer d'Entença, 57, Eixample; ///woods.rebounds.dampen;
www.cruixrestaurant.com

Valencian chef Miquel Pardo cooked all around Spain before opening Cruix in Eixample. It's here that locals book a table when they want to splash out on a swanky meal without blowing their entire month's salary. The very reasonable tasting menu is lined with fusion dishes, like hake churros with a salsa verde and Pardo's signature *fuet nigiri* (a Catalan salami). And, good news: Pardo stays true to his roots by including an excellent rice course (we'd expect nothing less from a chef hailing from the home of paella).

DOS PEBROTS

Map 2; Carrer del Dr Dou, 19, Raval; ///stubbed.sedated.racing; www.dospebrots.com

Embark on a voyage through time with chef Albert Raurich, who is quite the culinary historian. Each item on his menu is rooted in a point in Mediterranean history and reimagined to give it 21st-century flair (Raurich studied numerous books for research). Take the open-faced Roman omelette, prepared tableside with pine nuts and anchovy garum. The menu lists each dish's background so you and your pals will know precisely which decade you're chomping your way through.
» Don't leave without trying the Persian kebab (1,500 BCE), which you'll assemble yourself. Slow-cooked lamb and fresh pitta bread – joyous.

MONT BAR

Map 4; Carrer de la Diputació, 220, Eixample; ///info.limes.cotton; www.montbar.com

A lip-smacking selection of regional wines is paired with fresh takes on Catalan cuisine at this upscale bistro-style restaurant. Yes, these dishes are local at heart but prepared with a clear French pedigree and enhanced with international flavours; think cucumber carbonara, Cantonese suckling pig and cockle soufflé.

BERBENA

Map 4; Carrer de Minerva, 6, Gràcia; ///thick.fairness.ruins;
www.berbenabcn.com

Having worked in Michelin-star kitchens at home and abroad, local boy Carlos Pérez de Rozas left the world of fine dining and made his way back to Barna to do things on his own terms. Using seasonal ingredients, he reimagines Catalan classics, creating a menu that changes often. Check out the socials of local foodies, who regularly update their feeds with Berbena's latest offerings, for a sneak preview.

SUCULENT

Map 2; Rambla del Raval, 45, Raval; ///spoon.contacts.gather;
www.suculent.com

Best described as the lovechild of a French brasserie and Catalan grandma's kitchen, Suculent sits tucked away at the bottom of the Rambla del Raval. Here you'll find local chefs checking out the competition and hungry lunch-goers chatting loudly over one another, all keen to show their appreciation of the nose-to-tail cuisine.

BESTA

Map 4; Carrer d'Aribau, 106, Eixample; ///shorts.prelude.future;
www.bestabarcelona.com

Why limit your cooking to only one region when Spain's bounty stretches from coast to coast? This was the thinking of chefs Manu Núñez and Carles Ramon, the former from northwestern Galicia and the latter from here in Catalunya. Besta is a celebration of the two regions' cuisines, marrying the flavours of the Atlantic and the Mediterranean. The menu changes so often that if you come again you'll likely be greeted with something entirely different to tuck into.

TABERNA NOROESTE

Map 3; Carrer de Radas, 67, Poble Sec; ///zooms.troubled.boat; www.tabernanoroeste.com

Fire-roasted peppers with San Simón cheese and Cantabrian anchovies, Castilian-style suckling lamb with Galician potatoes: it's all about the flavours of the north and west of Spain at this ultra-hip spot. Scenesters know to ask for a table by the open kitchen where they can watch the chefs expertly prepare creative small plates.

EL CHIGRE 1769

Map 1; Carrer dels Sombrerers, 7, Born; ///probing.husbands.investor; www.elchigre1769.com

Nestled behind the medieval church of Santa Maria del Mar, in an 18th-century stone building, El Chigre is a glow-up of a traditional Asturian cider tavern. Yes, there are the ubiquitous heaps of fresh seafood on ice and bunches of garlic hanging from rustic ceiling beams. The dishes, though, are wholly refined; downsized and carefully crafted, creative plates include octopus doused with seaweed "chimichurri" sauce and prawns served on a bed of black rice.

» Don't leave without trying the Asturian cider, a very tart and non-carbonated drink that requires a specific pouring technique. Ask your server for a demo, or simply follow your neighbour's lead.

Veggie and Vegan

Long gone are the days when Barcelonan cooks slipped chunks of ham or chorizo into almost every dish. Today the city is a veritable cornucopia of meat-free offerings.

VEG WORLD INDIA

Map 4; Carrer de Bruniquer, 24, Gràcia; ///ruffle.kinks.turned; www.vegworldindiabarcelona.es

Gràcia locals jostle at the tables of this popular spot, tucking into steaming baskets of fresh naan (there are nine varieties), spicy bowls of chickpea chana masala and delicate paneer dosa. Most dishes on the 100 per cent vegetarian menu can be made vegan too (just ask). Opt for the "Indian Specialities" section of the menu for hearty helpings of *aloo gobi* (potato and cauliflower curry) and *bhindi baji* okra.

RABIPELAO

Map 4; Carrer del Torrent d'En Vidalet 22, Gràcia; ///skipped.foal.flicks; www.elrabipelao.com

Sometimes the strangest combinations work the best. Take Rabipelao: a dining room decked out like a British neo-Victorian cabaret that plates up veggie and vegan takes on Venezuelan classics, like *arepas* (stuffed cornmeal patties) and *tequeños* (cheese-filled fried breadsticks). Treating a friend for their birthday? Order the sharing platter and prepare to gorge yourselves on every dish on the menu.

» Don't leave without rounding off your feast of a meal with a flaming mai tai out on Rabipelao's shabby-chic patio.

FLAX & KALE
Map 5; Carrer de Sant Pere Més Alt, 31, 33, Sant Pere;
///minerals.invented.shady; www.flaxandkale.com

Brainchild of Catalan chef and plant-based pioneer Teresa Carles, Flax & Kale is technically flexitarian so you'll see a smattering of dairy, eggs and fish on the menu. Glaze over this and instead head straight for the list of wood-fired pizzas, which are entirely vegan, gluten-free and, quite frankly, to die for (even if you're a total cheese fiend). Try the vegan truffle pizza with coconut cream, wild mushrooms and truffle oil — trust us, it's sublime.

Shh!

Hidden away between Raval and Sant Antoni, hole-in-the-wall bar Jonny Aldana serves up Latin American vegan fast food *(www.jonnyaldana.com)*. Clubbers often call in at the night-time only bar to fuel up on tasty meat-free nachos and tacos, though you could easily pop in here even if you're not heading out on the town. With good food and vibes, the night's plans are inevitably forgotten — why move on?

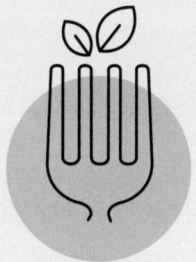

Liked by the locals

"Arriving in the 2000s, the best a vegan could expect was a stare of incomprehension. Now the scene is completely different. Many restaurants offer dishes like fermented black bean salsa brava, tempeh chicken burgers, veggie fast food and vegan jackfruit tacos."

BÉATRIX LUJUA, FOOD WRITER AND CHEF

L'HORTET

**Map 2; Carrer del Pintor Fortuny 32, Raval; ///fixated.cowboys.deals;
www.restaurantvegetariahortet.com**

Barcelona's original plant-based point of reference, L'Hortet has been
serving workers from the *barri* for some 40 years now. The bistro only
opens for lunchtime and serves up fixed-price, three-course veggie
meals of hearty soups, stews and meat-free takes on Catalan classics.

ROOTS & ROLLS

**Map 5; Carrer del Consell de Cent, 401, Eixample;
///appear.changes.shades; www.rootsandrolls.com**

Uber-stylish Roots & Rolls is the go-to place for a working lunch.
Chew over that latest project while enjoying vegan Japanese
comfort foods such as gyoza and *okonomiyaki* (savoury pancakes),
or perhaps some plant-based sushi.

» Don't leave without sampling "Heura", the soya-based chicken
substitute that was invented right here in Barcelona.

FAT VEGGIES

**Map 4; Carrer de Bailèn, 81, Eixample; ///villa.clip.sneezed;
www.fatveggies.com**

The philosophy at Fat Veggies is that good ol' vegetables deserve
to be more than just humble side-dishes: here, they're the stars of
the show. Seared, smoked, charred or fermented, the seasonal
produce is meticulously prepared with flavours that are entirely
Mediterranean (think carrots doused in a tomato-rich sauce).

Cheap Eats

When it comes to cheap and cheerful bites, Barna delivers. Locals graze on sandwiches for elevenses (brunch isn't a thing here), gobble quick lunches and gorge on gourmet burgers before a night of partying.

BODEGA MONTFERRY

Map 6; Passatge de Serra i Arola, 13, Sants;
///riders.shakes.stubborn; www.bodegamontferrysants.com

This tapas spot may have been around since the 1960s, but it's kept with the times: the sandwich of the day draws loyal followers daily, keen to try the latest sarnie combo. The menu doesn't stop at mouth-watering sandwiches, either; there are plenty of delicious, hearty dishes served here for under €10 daily. It's no wonder its fans keep coming back for more.

RAMEN-YA HIRO

Map 4; Carrer de Girona 164, Gràcia; ///speaking.pleasing.tides;
www.ramenyahiro.com

People never queue for a restaurant in Barcelona (life's way too short), unless that restaurant is Ya Hiro. And what are they waiting for? Chef Hiroki Yoshiyuki's sublime ramen, that's what. Hiroki

If you're too hungry to queue, but still fancy Japanese food, try Yoi Yoi Gion, just a few minutes away.

spent years fine-tuning the recipe and watches over the pot of bubbling broth for hours each day. With patience comes pure perfection.

FUNKY BAKERS DELI

Map 5; Carrer de la Diputació, 347, Eixample; ///shields.supply.quirky; www.funkybakers.com

What began as a small bakery and take-away window on the Passeig del Born has grown, thanks to huge demand, into this second, larger bakery and café. Founder Seyma's Turkish roots are merged with food traditions from around Europe; braided challah bread and cardamom babkas share menu space with Danish-style smørrebrød and wickedly creamy Basque cheesecake.

» Don't leave without sampling the *borek*, a savoury, slightly spicy Turkish pastry of coiled filo dough stuffed with potatoes and herbs.

MANTEQUERÍAS PIRENAICAS

Map 6; Carrer de Muntaner, 460, Sarrià-Sant Gervasi; ///hours.liberty.declares; 932 019 189

Remember: Catalans eat lunch around 2pm, after which it's siesta time. Too peckish to wait until then? Head to this cheery little spot around noon for an *aperitiu* (small bite before a meal) before the staff snap the doors shut and mosey on home for a bite to eat and a snooze. A *canya* (small beer), *flauta* (mini sandwich) and olives to share amid the loud chatter will make you feel like a true Barcelonan.

LA BIKINERIA

Map 4; Carrer de Mallorca, 135, Eixample; ///dots.risen.monument;
www.labikineria.es

Here in Barcelona, a *bikini* isn't just a piece of swimwear, it's also a cheese-and-ham toastie. This staple snack is found at almost every bar and café but La Bikineria is the one place that takes the humble *bikini* to a whole new level, using delicious gourmet ingredients. We're talking things like black sausage and oozy brie.

FALAFEL SHEL SHANI

Map 2; La Rambla, 91, Mercat de la Boqueria, 133–134, Raval;
///unites.tweeted.cotton; www.falafelboqueria.com

La Boqueria market *(p109)* has loads of restaurants that serve up the bounty of the city, but that bounty is rarely vegan. Enter Falafel Shel Shani, the handiwork of Israeli cook Shani Waytzman. Expect hot and fluffy pitta stuffed with fresh falafel (Shani learned the recipe from her father), your choice of toppings (thin slices of fried aubergine are our favourite), and lashings of tahini and chilli oil. Gluten-free and kosher options are also available.

CONESA

Map 1; Carrer de la Llibreteria, 1, Gothic Quarter;
///routines.fires.emblem; www.conesaentrepans.com

The bustling square that houses the City Council and Catalan government has been home to another crucial institution for the last 60 years: Conesa. Barcelona's oldest sandwich joint continues to bring in droves of partygoers, all looking to line their stomachs with hearty baguettes before going big on nights out. Vegans and coeliacs, have no fear: there's a number of offerings for you, too.

» **Don't leave without** grabbing one of the filled wasabi bread baguettes and finding a spot on Plaça de Sant Miquel to eat it.

COMPÁ

Map 5; Carrer de Sant Carles, 19, Barceloneta; ///shark.unwell.branch; 623 312 282

After a morning sunning themselves on Barceloneta's beaches, bronzed locals have one place in mind: the tiny deli counter of Compá. Here Vittorio Cicero does his homeland of Calabria proud, whipping up paninis laden with juicy pork meatballs, spicy nduja sausage, long-simmered tomato sauce and loads of molten cheese. Panini devoured, it's straight back to the beach to bask in a food coma.

CONSERVAS LATORRE

Map 3; Carrer de Calàbria 57, Sant Antoni; ///sobbed.loudly.feeds; 660 915 633

Forget what you think you know about canned goods: in Spain, tinned seafood delights aren't left to collect dust at the back of kitchen cupboards, they're celebrated. And there's no better place to enjoy all things tinned than at Conservas Latorre. Let the friendly waiters guide you to the best dishes, which all centre on preserved specialities. Hungry for more? Then let them recommend the best tins to take home with you.

Tapear

"Tapear", or "to go for tapas", is key to city life. Unlike elsewhere in Spain, you won't get free tapas with your drink in Barcelona. Locals instead pay for the privilege to enjoy these tasty morsels.

BAR DEL PLA

Map 1; Carrer de Montcada, 2, Born; ///lavender.ally.pockets; www.bardelpla.cat

Tapas is given a dose of nostalgia at Bar del Pla, where seasonal specials are paired with what the staff lovingly call *plats de la iaia* (grandma dishes). These old-school Catalan dishes include beef cheeks in red wine, smoked sardine flatbreads and pig trotters.

BAR ALEGRÍA

Map 3; Carrer del Comte Borrell, 133, Sant Antoni; ///thus.belonging.festivity; www.baralegriarestaurante.com

"Alegría" means joy and the staff at this lively *Modernista* bar certainly do the name justice. You'll likely hear your waiter bellow at the bar, asking for your *canya* (small glass of beer), to be met by smart retorts. On the food front, expect tapas with a twist. Written on a blackboard, the 15 or so dishes use top-quality ingredients and you'll see just how exceptionally well these are put to use after your first bite. If you're lucky, a bunch of musicians will show up to entertain the crowd in true Alegría style. Like we said: pure joy.

BAR JAI-CA

Map 5; Carrer de Ginebra, 13, Barceloneta; ///slab.pony.weeded; www.barjaica.com

Welcome to one of Barceloneta's classics, a bar that was once so raucous it landed the owner with an 18-month prison sentence for noise pollution. Things have calmed down a bit since then, but Bar Jai-Ca still has one of the liveliest atmospheres in the city, thanks to its regular crowd of tipsy good-timers and bronzed beachgoers, all chowing down on succulent seafood tapas.

LA ALCOBA AZUL

Map 1; Carrer de Salomó ben Adret, 14, Gothic Quarter; ///exposing.pints.tweaked; www.laalcobaazul.com

The tight, winding streets of Barcelona's old Jewish Quarter have an otherworldly magic about them. Nowhere epitomizes this more than La Alcoba Azul, a candlelit cave hidden in the heart of the *barri*. Couples cosy up at rickety tables, talking in hushed whispers as jazz music plays softly in the background. They're here for the bar's irresistible experimental tapas, like cod carpaccio and spiced baked tomatoes, which they pair with the bar's potent cocktails.

» Don't leave without sharing a classic Catalan dinner of *torrades* – large slices of toast piled high with a range of different treats.

Solo, Pair, Crowd

Whether you're meeting new people, on a date or making merry with the gang, *tapear* is all about socializing.

FLYING SOLO
Mingle with the locals
Sant Antoni's Bodega d'en Rafael is as local as it gets. Staff will ask you to tick what you want from a list of tapas before they go back to bantering with the regulars.

IN A PAIR
Swanky tapas for two
Date on the horizon? Make a beeline for Viblioteca in Gràcia. A play on *vino* (wine) and *biblioteca* (library), Viblioteca does exactly what it says on the tin (or, er, bottle). Pluck a bottle from the shelves and enjoy with some seriously refined tapas.

FOR A CROWD
Get the party started
Your elbow will touch your neighbour's at buzzy La Bicicleta (you and your pals will likely make a whole new posse of friends). Fab vibes aside, this favourite spot promises classic Catalan tapas at reasonable prices.

BODEGA LA PUNTUAL

Map 1; Carrer de Montcada, 22, Born; ///unstable.tune.gathers;
www.grupovarela.es/bodega-la-puntual-barcelona

This bodega was made for family gatherings. Expect to find big groups here: siblings laughing over glasses of vermouth, their kids greedily tucking into classic tapas and the grandparents inspecting the displays of cured meats and cheeses. Jolly and relaxed, this is what *tapeo* is all about.

BANYS VERGE DEL CARME

Map 6; Carrer del Mar, 4B, Montgat; ///expires.headed.folders;
www.banysvergedelcarme.com

Nothing beats eating tapas by the sea, the wind in your hair. Standing among the bathing huts on Montgat beach, this summertime shack is the perfect place for just that. Enjoy a beer and some seafood tapas before dipping your toe in the sea.

» Don't leave without trying the *cazón en adobo*, marinated and deep-fried dogfish (you won't want to share).

BODEGA AMPOSTA

Map 3; Carrer d'Amposta, 1, Sants; ///gravest.author.resemble;
www.bodegaamposta.com

With old wooden beams and polished marble surfaces, this outpost has all the reassuring trappings of a traditional tapas bar. But old-school, it is not. Brothers and owners Jordi and Josep give classic tapas a haute-cuisine flourish. The tasting menu is a great place to start.

Special Occasion

Entering a new decade? Secured that promotion? Put a ring on it? Barcelona might be a casual city but it's got a glut of restaurants that promise the glamour and gravitas that your big day deserves.

SAN PEDRITO

Map 1; Carrer de la Fusina, 6, Born; ///recent.disputes.national; www.sanpedritobcn.com

Sometimes a celebration calls for tacos and, thankfully, Mexican joint San Pedrito is there for those moments. Moody lighting, fiery salsas and plenty of top-shelf mezcal make for the perfect jubilant meal. Clink glasses of smoky *espadín* with friends on the outdoor terrace, or enjoy a romantic one-on-one meal in the cosy dining room. Whatever the occasion, San Pedrito promises a fiesta.

LE CUCINE MANDAROSSO

Map 1; Carrer de Verdaguer i Callís 4, Born; ///slicer.monkeys.curve; www.mandarosso.com

Walls stocked with gourmet ingredients, menus written up on black-boards and families chatting animatedly: Le Cucine Mandarosso has all the hallmarks of a picture-postcard Italian restaurant. As for the food, rest assured it's the full trattoria fantasy with recipes sourced from the owner's inner circle of Italian *nonnas*. Night-time is best for a relaxed à la carte meal with your nearest and dearest (the very reasonable set-menu lunch can make the place a little frantic).

» Don't leave without strolling round the corner to peruse the restaurant's emporium, stocked with all the finest goods from Italy.

CHERIFF

Map 5; Carrer de Ginebra, 15, Barceloneta; ///massive.bind.shots; www.cheriffrestaurant.es

Barceloneta isn't all gaudy tourist traps, and stylish Cheriff is a case in point. Step inside to discover mid-century design, soft lighting and a blow-out seafood menu. It's all about the stranger delights of Spanish seafood (think gooseneck barnacles and sea cucumbers), ideal for a celebratory meal with a difference.

BAR CAÑETE

Map 2; Carrer de la Unió, 17, Raval; ///keeps.bicker.sheets; www.barcanete.com

Cañete gets overlooked by locals thanks to its location in Raval, where anything vaguely upmarket tends to be a bit touristy. Yet this oh-so-charming tapas bar is second-to-none for a birthday banquet. Choose between the buzzy area called Barra (meaning "bar"), where parties of cheerful pals mingle at stand-up tables, and the swankier sit-down section Mantel (meaning "tablecloth"). Wherever you park up, sharing plates of tapas with loved ones is just the ticket for a special occasion.

ROBATA

Map 4; Carrer d'Enric Granados, 55, Eixample;
///margin.reserved.pretty; www.robata.es

Enric Granados is *the* go-to street in the Eixample – you heard it here
first. And though there are countless great spots here, Japanese
restaurant Robata is hard to beat. The sushi and grills are exceptional,
the sticky chicken wings are to die for, and the cheesecake (off-brand,
we know) is out of this world. Add a selection of sakes (staff will talk
you through them) and you'll be raving about Robata for weeks.

CINC SENTITS

Map 3; Carrer d'Entença, 60, Eixample; ///melons.piles.parties;
www.cincsentits.com

Looking for the meal of a lifetime? Look no further. At Cinc Sentits,
chef Jordi Artal cooks a menu deeply rooted in Catalan tradition
but with a wholly modern approach. The 10-course tasting menu at
his two-Michelin-starred restaurant coaxes out flavours and aromas
from the very best products of the season. If you're feeling really
fancy, splash out on the wine pairings.

TERRAZA MARTÍNEZ

Map 3; Carretera de Miramar, 38, Montjuïc; ///helpful.mint.mimed;
www.martinezbarcelona.com

A special occasion deserves a special view, and nowhere can outdo
Terraza Martínez when it comes to scenery. Suited-and-booted locals
gaze out at the city, shoreline and mountains at this gorgeous spot,

After a paella feast? Remember that it's a lunchtime affair; locals never, ever eat paella for dinner.

plopped on the northeastern face of Montjuïc. The menu is a hit, too, with rich paellas, oysters and fresh fish – the perfect feast to celebrate, well, anything.

SILAN

Map 4; Carrer d'Enric Granados, 38, Eixample;
///deflect.typhoon.chop; 930 315 816

Why not save the celebration for morning? Kick off the day in style with a smashingly good brunch at Silan. The Middle Eastern bistro throngs with trendy crowds, all inhaling the fragrant punch of sumac and cumin wafting up from platters of shakshuka and beef kebabs. After you've feasted, sit back with another coffee and enjoy a heart-to-heart with your favourite people – the day is young, after all.

» **Don't leave without** tucking into the oblong Jerusalem bagel, baked that day and served with tahini, Moroccan olives and zaatar.

ESTIMAR

Map 1; Carrer de Sant Antoni dels Sombrerers, 3, Born;
///helpers.supper.mistaken; www.restaurante-estimar.com

The day's catch is displayed on ice like a centrepiece at this temple to seafood. Our top tip? If money is no object (wouldn't that be nice?), this is the place to sample some of Spain's luxury items, like barnacles harvested from the stormy coastline of Galicia. A more humble (and wallet-friendly) dish is the fried baby squid served with inky black mayo.

Raise a glass at
REKONS

Stop to *vermutea* ("drink vermouth")
and chomp on an Argentine empanada at
Rekons. The puff pastry is second to none.

4

CARRER DEL

CARRER DE

CARRER

FLORIDABLANCA

COMTE BORRELL

CARRER DEL COMTE D'URGELL

RONDA DE SANT ANTONI

RONDA

SANT
ANTONI

Finish up at
BAR RAMÓN

5

Ramón Estalella opened this cheery joint in 1939.
Swing by to say *hola* to his grandkids who are busy
keeping his legacy alive. Faded posters of jazz
stars line the walls, rock 'n' roll plays overhead and
the regulars tuck into crowd-pleasing tapas.

*Once an open-air food
market targeted at
hungry commuters,
today the now-covered*
Mercat de Sant Antoni
is a social hub.

CARRER DE VILADOMAT

CARRER DE TAMARIT

Soak up some history at
BAR CALDERS

Catalan author Pere Calders took refuge in these
walls during the Civil War. Today Sant Antoni locals
pack out the bar and its terrace, tucking into traditional
tapas and Mexican specialities. Arrive early (around
6pm) to secure a spot.

2

CARRER DEL PARLAMENT

CARRER DE MANSO

Fortify yourself at
BAR BODEGA GOL

Sit down for a bite at this
old school sports bar, favoured by
Sant Antoni locals for its traditional yet
elevated plates of stews and fried fish.

1

| 0 metres | 100 |
| 0 yards | 100 |

AVINGUDA DEL PARAL·LEL

CARRER DE LA RIERA ALTA

CARRER DE SANT ANTONI ABAT

SANT PAU

3 **Graze at**
ELS SORTIDORS
DEL PARLAMENT
Continue on to this buzzy bodega, where fancy tapas await. Our top pick? That's the quail egg and black truffle oil omelette.

AVINGUDA DEL PARAL·LEL

An evening of
tapas in Sant Antoni

Time spent in Barcelona isn't complete without an evening *tapeando* ("eating tapas"). Sitting next to Raval and Poble Sec, Sant Antoni – Barna's best-kept secret – is just the place for a bite-sized feast. The charming *barri* dates back to the 15th century but it was the opening of a food market, in 1882, that made Sant Antoni what it is today: a foodie hotspot where locals actually know one another's names. Expect family-run tapas bars, cosy bodegas and a warm welcome.

1. Bar Bodega Gol
Carrer del Parlament 10;
689 33 24 00
///locals.belonging.chat

2. Bar Calders
Carrer del Parlament, 25;
933 299 349
///harvest.timidly.trifle

3. Els Sortidors del Parlament
Carrer del Parlament, 53;
934 411 602
///sliding.raft.limes

4. Rekons
Carrer del Comte d'Urgell, 32; www.empanadasrekons.com
///rice.lofts.combos

5. Bar Ramón
Carrer del Comte Borrell, 81;
www.barramon.dudaone.com
///strapped.noting.birds

Mercat de Sant Antoni
///hotdog.drivers.sparkle

DRINK

Locals live their lives in Barna's bodegas, vermuterias and cafés. Cocktails are sipped on date night, beers are clinked after work and coffees are savoured at weekends.

Vermouth Bars

Vermouth is more than a drink (a fortified wine, to be precise), it's a social occasion. On your travels through Barna you'll likely hear the phrase "fer el vermut", meaning to have an aperitif with a light snack.

BODEGA MARÍN

Map 4; Carrer de Milà i Fontanals, 72, Gràcia; ///exact.clever.suspend; www.bodegamarin.com

Impossibly narrow and bursting with bottles and barrels, this tiny bodega is a kitschy time capsule from another era. Gràcia locals (*graciencs*, to those in the know) inspect the curious decor – a lifetime of old photos, commemorative plates, handwritten notes and novelty calendars from years gone by – all while sipping the no-frills house vermouth served straight from the barrel.

MORRO FI

Map 3; Carrer del Consell de Cent, 171, Eixample; ///unveils.chef.trap; www.morrofi.cat

Remember when blogs were a thing? That's how Morro Fi began: a blog run by friends celebrating all that made Barcelona's traditional bars tick. Years of painstaking research transformed into a real-life bar, Morro Fi, which soon became the city's vermouth bar *par excellence* despite being the size of a postage stamp. It's so popular that you'll spot Morro Fi's house-made vermouth across the city.

LAS VERMUDAS

Map 4; Carrer del Robí, 32, Gràcia; ///cattle.dabble.prone; www.lasvermudas.com

Vermouth bars can be a traditional affair (we're looking at you Bodega E. Marín) but that's not the case at Las Vermudas, with its tropical decor and innovative cocktails (vermouth-based, naturally). Four friends – Andrea, Elena, Filippo and Rafael – established this Gràcia bar, today serving up their own takes on the city staple.

SENYOR VERMUT

Map 4; Carrer de Provença, 85, Eixample; ///complain.hamster.booklet; 935 328 865

If you happen to be walking through Eixample around midday at the weekend (in other words, prime vermouth time), you'll no doubt be drawn to Senyor Vermut. Punters spill out of the bar and onto the street corner, supping vermouth and chatting with uncharacteristic levels of conviviality for Barcelona. Inside you'll find row upon row of vermouth bottles, plus the owner's collection of antique seltzer bottles – another crucial element for a classic vermouth aperitif.

>> Don't leave without sampling Senyor Vermut's *patatas bravas*, which locals claim are some of the best in the city thanks to the extra spicy sauce (or at least extra spicy by Catalan tastes).

Solo, Pair, Crowd

Whatever the occasion or number in your squad, there's a glut of lovely spots to clink a glass of vermouth.

FLYING SOLO

People-watch with a drink

Stop off for a glass of vermouth in this historic bar that's been here for over 100 years. Nestled down a Raval side street, facing what's left of the crumbling arches of the Church of Saint Augustine, it's an ideal spot from which to watch the world go by.

IN A PAIR

Chat among the bottles

Hidden away on one of the Gothic Quarter's alleyways, La Cala del Vermut is an intimate spot to enjoy a natter and an aperitif amid all the bottles on sale. Why not buy one for later, too?

FOR A CROWD

A barrel of laughs

Forget booking a table for the whole gang – gather everyone around a barrel or two at Bodega Vinito in Sant Antoni instead. You'll all truly feel like locals.

LA VERMU

Map 4; Carrer de Sant Domènec, 15, Gràcia; ///mascot.rocks.twists;
www.lavermu.es

Popular any day of the week, La Vermu buzzes with colleagues gathering for an after-work drink and friends meeting for an aperitif. Whatever the occasion, traditional *embutits* (cured meats and tinned seafood) and creative tapas (like marinated bluefin tuna) are paired with obligatory glasses of vermouth.

VERMUTERIA LA LOLA

Map 3; Carrer del Consell de Cent, 82, Eixample; ///fizzle.credited.launched

Sure, its decor might not have been updated since the 1980s, but what makes La Lola special is its mixed bag of neighbourhood residents, from vermouth-quaffing hipsters to *abuelas* with their dinky lapdogs. Join them on the bar's southwest-facing terrace, perfect for catching the midday sun.

» Don't leave without checking out the tapas under the bar's glass counter – perfect for soaking up that second vermouth.

TRENCALÒS

Map 6; Carrer del Vallespir 73, Sants; ///shack.galaxies.slumped; 930 163 115

A ski-themed vermouth bar with mountain equipment arranged across the walls: an odd concept, but somehow it works. No need to pretend you know anything about Barcelona's favourite tipple here; the charming staff will be more than happy to advise you on the bar's huge range of vermouths.

Bodegas and Wine Bars

Old-school wine bars (bodegas) and their modern counterparts are central to the city's cultural heritage. This is where locals debrief on their day with a glass of wine, or fill up a bottle from the barrel to take home.

BAR SALVATGE

Map 4; Carrer de Verdi, 50, Gràcia; ///sobbed.totally.mattress; www.barsalvatge.com

"Natural wines from wild winemakers" is the ethos at this hip Gràcia bar. The good people of Salvatge aren't concerned with a wine's prestige. They're more interested in the peculiar flavours that the natural winemaking process can conjure; the more obscure the better.

MACOT

Map 6; Carrer de Violant d'Hongria Reina d'Aragó, 150, Sants; ///loudly.curable.coconut; www.macotbaravins.com

Macot is *the* home of slow food and slow wine. For such a tiny spot, it has a surprisingly extensive wine list to choose from, shining a light on natural wines sourced from small producers across Europe. The

Don't forget to order one of Macot's famous brioche sandwiches to pair with all that wine.

glasses are poured (and refilled) alongside a menu of seasonal small bites – the perfect pairing for a leisurely end to the day.

BODEGA MANOLO

Map 6; Carrer del Torrent de les Flors, 101, Gràcia; ///grin.hello.migrate; 932 844 377

History is palpable at Bodega Manolo. The smell of damp, wine-soaked wood fills the air and the furnishings remain much as they were 100 years ago. With the vibe of a welcoming working men's club, the bodega is a far cry from the city's bougier wine bars, and all the better for it. See for yourself why locals are so loyal to the Gràcia institution and head here for a glass of well-aged, full-bodied red.

ZONA D'OMBRA

Map 1; Carrer de Salomó ben Adret, 12, Gothic Quarter; ///gateway.booth.figure; www.zonadombra.es

In the heart of the Gothic Quarter, this unassuming wine bar doubles as a bottle shop specializing in regional and Spanish labels. Yes, you can pop in and buy a bottle to take home, but why not draw up a chair and sample a couple of the two-dozen wines available by the glass? There's also a selection of tapas, artisan cheeses and crusty bread that will stop you from leaving completely sozzled.

» Don't leave without ordering the tasting flight. For around the same price as a single glass you can sample three wines.

BAR BODEGA QUIMET

Map 4; Carrer de Vic, 23, Gràcia; ///drivers.sailors.cages; 932 184 189

The good people of Gràcia gravitate towards Bar Bodega Quimet for its good value lunch menu and old-world charm. The barrels on the walls aren't for show; wines are dispensed by the glass and litre for prices so cheerful that you might mistake them for typos. But don't call this spot "cheap" – it's one of the few remaining places where the quality-to-price ratio is still in favour of guests.

>> Don't leave without trying the famous octopus, an entire "arm" that's slowly simmered, charred and served with silky potato purée.

BODEGA MAESTRAZGO

Map 5; Carrer de Sant Pere Més Baix, 90, Born;
///ventures.singled.voting; 933 102 673

We all know that wine only gets better with time, and Bodega Maestrazgo is in itself a fine vintage. It's been in the same family for over 60 years and current owner José has three generations of wine knowledge to back him up. Swing by to pick his brains.

Try it!
WINE TASTINGS

José will teach you how to guzzle with confidence at a Bodega Maestrazgo tasting session. He focuses on Spanish wines, so you'll be able to show off your knowledge next time someone brings a Rioja to dinner.

CELLER CAL MARINO

Map 3; Carrer de Margarit, 54, Poble Sec; ///making.spurned.sides;
www.calmarino.tumblr.com

Once a fizzy drink factory, then a motorbike workshop, today Celler
Cal Marino is filled to the rafters with barrels of wine. In true Barna
style, empties are converted into makeshift tables. And gathered
round them? Thirsty locals working to finish off the next barrel.

ELS SORTIDORS DEL PARLAMENT

Map 3; Carrer del Parlament, 53, Sant Antoni; ///sliding.raft.limes;
934 411 602

After clocking off for the day, office and home workers make for
the ultra-cool bars on Parlament, a favourite of which is this snug
bodega. Els Sortidors de Parlament brings together the rustic
charm of an old winery with all the services of a modern wine bar.
Buy a bottle to-go or bag a barrel and enjoy a glass or two in-house
(for a small corkage fee).

CAN CISA

Map 1; Carrer de la Princesa, 14, Born; ///cubes.flasks.backs;
www.barbrutal.com

One of the premier natural wine bars in the city, if not Spain, Can
Cisa is the front half of upscale restaurant Bar Brutal. Every week,
unique, natural and "living" wines from around the world arrive at
Can Cisa, and special events are held in their honour (we're talking
bar takeovers, pop-up chef events and boozy brunch specials).

Coffee Shops

*Like all other Europeans, Barcelonans love a
good cup of coffee. And though the craze for ultra-hip
coffee shops has really taken hold, the locals still
cherish the city's quality old-school spots, too.*

SLOWMOV
**Map 4; Carrer de Neptú, 36, Gràcia, ///entire.stealing.barman;
www.slowmov.com**

As the name implies, SlowMov is hailed as the coffee version of the
slow food movement. Step into this airy space for a quick dose of
caffeine and, before you know it, you'll have spent an hour watching
the baristas expertly grind the single-origin beans and craft frothy latte
art. An unhurried coffee here really is the perfect pick-me-up.

BAR LA CAMILA
**Map 4; Carrer de Banyoles, 11, Gràcia;
///withdrew.parkway.uses; 932 498 891**

When two local coffee aficionados, Clara and María, opened
Bar La Camila in 2022, they decided to step back from the popular
minimalist coffee shop aesthetic often found across the city. Instead,
their little drink stop is set up in the style of a typical Catalan bar, but

 Feeling peckish?
There are plenty
of light bites on offer
– perfect with coffee
or wine.

with an effortlessly cool, mid-century twist. Join loyal Gràcia locals and sip on a warm brew – or a *vermut*, come evening – and feel oh-so stylish.

CAFÉS EL MAGNÍFICO

Map 1; Carrer de l'Argenteria, 64, Born; ///protests.texted.entry; www.cafeselmagnifico.com

Regulars have been sipping their java at El Magnífico since the 1980s when Salvador Sans opened this roastery. Sure, it might not have the style of other cafés in Barna but the coffee is top-quality and freshly ground. Expect your cappuccino to arrive in chunky china with a little biscuit on the side – just like it would have in the 80s.

» Don't leave without sampling the *shakerato* (essentially espresso shaken over ice). It feels like a cocktail but it's perfectly acceptable for breakfast and great during the hotter months.

FEDERAL CAFÉ

Map 3; Carrer del Parlament, 39, Sant Antoni; ///sunk.belonged.archives; 931 873 607

Federal owes its name to a small town in New South Wales, and though this Sant Antoni coffee spot gives a flavour of Oz (think avocado on toast with perfectly poached eggs, washed down with a flat white), the place is wholly European in feel. Two floors of sleek wooden furnishings, stylish locals, scattered books and magazines, plus a lovely roof garden – you could be in Amsterdam or Copenhagen.

NEWS & COFFEE

Map 5; Passeig de Sant Joan, 17, Eixample; ///tailed.dodges.skin;
www.newsandcoffee.eu

The fun folk of News & Coffee have given four old, dusty newspaper stands the hipster treatment, kitting them out with indie magazines and top-of-the-line coffee machines. Behind the counters, beanie-wearing baristas skilfully pour speciality coffees to-go and dish out zine recommends (their motto is "if you don't like to read, you haven't found the right magazine"). Just down the road from Parc de la Ciutadella (p176), the stand in Eixample is our favourite.

ON Y VA

Map 6; Carrer de Cornet i Mas, 9, Sarrià-Sant Gervasi;
///blame.snows.sanded; www.onyvacoffee.com

Coffee connoisseur and keen cyclist Ferran Buxeda is the brains behind On y va (which means "let's go" in French). Ferran knows exactly what his fellow cyclists need on a bike ride stop-off: strong speciality coffees and tasty snacks to keep them pedalling, not to mention a wonderful sense of community.

DEPARTURE COFFEE

Map 2; Carrer de la Verge, 1, Raval; ///magma.vertical.boldest;
935 630 589

This little spot is almost impossible to stumble across, hidden as it is down a small side street mere minutes from the overwhelming roads of Raval. Though its industrial-chic décor may suggest otherwise, this isn't a paradise for freelancers and digital nomads: there's a strict no-laptop policy. Instead, it's a tranquil spot to sit back and enjoy a leisurely brew before a busy day of sightseeing or shopping.

» **Don't leave without** crossing the street to visit Lata Peinada *(p94)*, a bookshop with a stellar selection of Latin American literature.

SYRA

Map 4; Carrer de la Mare de Déu dels Desemparats, 8, Gràcia; ///kindest.pastime.payout; www.syracoffee.com

Barcelonans know that Gràcia's many squares are perfect for settling down with a coffee and indulging in a bit of people-watching. And Syra, a little hole-in-the-wall café, provides people with the perfect coffee for these moments. Single-origin, freshly roasted, aromatic: the coffee here is sublime, especially when paired with delicious treats like baklava and carrot cake.

NOMAD COFFEE LAB

Map 5; Passatge Sert, 12, Sant Pere; ///sensible.sunk.organs; www.nomadcoffee.es

No mention of coffee in Barcelona is complete without a nod to Nomad, one of the pioneers in the city's speciality coffee movement. The first of three branches, the Nomad Coffee Lab is nestled in a pretty, plant-filled passage in the upper reaches of Sant Pere. Here, founder Jordi Mestre and his team test and serve their newest and most special beans, sourced responsibly from farmers across the world.

Characterful Bars

Looking for a watering hole with a difference? Tucked down the city's ancient streets, these characterful boozers – plus their quirky owners and eccentric decor – promise a story with your drink.

LONDON BAR

Map 2; Carrer Nou de la Rambla, 34, Raval; ///outpost.nursery.wedge; 938 082 187

When London Bar opened in the 1910s, the aim was to imitate a British pub and give punters like Dalí and Picasso (both regulars) a taste of the English capital. But something must have been lost in translation. Instead of the low wooden beams, leather armchairs and bar taps that are synonymous with British boozers, the place is a hodgepodge of Art Deco decor and fancy cocktails. This doesn't stop Barcelonans from popping in for a knees-up, mind.

BAR LEO

Map 5; Carrer de Sant Carles, 34, Barceloneta; ///milder.outdone.pastime

It might have been open for just 40 years but locals say you're not a true Barcelonan until you've stepped inside Bar Leo. You'll be greeted by the warm smile of owner Leocadia and the trill of rumba music (plus posters of flamenco legend Bambino peeling on the walls). Like an Andalucian mother, Leocadia will insist you try her *tortilla de patatas* and *banderillas* (a cocktail stick of olives, pepper and anchovies) as well as an obligatory vermouth. Don't leave anything on your plate – she'll be back to check that you enjoyed every item.

LA CONCHA

Map 2; Carrer de Guàrdia, 14, Raval; ///places.builder.galaxies; 933 024 118

Actor and singer Sara Montiel was one of the few gay icons of Francoist Spain and this LGBTQ+ bar is dedicated to her memory. Every wall is plastered with portraits of the fearless diva, Spain's first Hollywood star who spoke out passionately for gender equality. Montiel passed away in 2013 but her spirit lives on at La Concha.

BAR MARSELLA

Map 2; Carrer de Sant Pau, 65, Raval; ///recoup.gold.warm

Dating back to 1820, Bar Marsella became notorious in the 1920s when artists and bohemians sipped absinthe here to fuel their creativity. The beloved haunt has barely been cleaned since those days; pre-Civil War bottles line the walls, the ceiling is stained with cigarette smoke and the chandeliers are thick with cobwebs. Add the surly nature of the owner and you'll feel like you've fallen into a ghost story. Or perhaps that's just the influence of the green fairy.

» Don't leave without settling your stomach after all that absinthe by stumbling over to La Monroe de la Filmo for some delicious tapas.

BARETO OLÍMPIC

Map 2; Carrer de Joaquín Costa, 25, Raval;
///bespoke.rods.clues

Oh, the 80s! A decade of hedonistic partying, Freddie Mercury and pre-Olympic fever. It was all this that inspired the opening of Bar Olímpic in the late 80s when the city was gearing up for the 1992 Olympics. Today good-timers come here for the tasty cocktails and revelrous vibes. Seriously, you'll be singing Freddie and Montserrat's "Barcelona" before your second beer.

BAR RAÏM

Map 4; Carrer de Siracusa, 4, Gràcia; ///sensible.loves.escape; 687 459 679

The region of Catalunya has a shady colonial history. Take the rum trade: everyone's go-to rum, Bacardí, was created by an *indià*, the name given to Catalans who made their fortune in the Caribbean, particularly in Cuba. Bar Raïm is all about spotlighting this dark patch of local history, with black-and-white photographs and Cuban flags plastered across its walls, all to remind locals of the past.

BAR PASTÍS

Map 2; Carrer de Santa Mònica, 4, Raval; ///steadily.loads.encoded;
619 753 740

Slip into the world of French writer Jean Genet at Pastís. This dinky 1940s bar was once a favourite with cabaret-goers and French exiles, such as Genet, who lived here in Barna. It's still got that feel of the Raval underworld, thanks to the portraits of bohemians, yellowing newspaper cuttings and the incongruous pair of plastic legs sporting can-can stockings (ripped, naturally). As for drinks, Gallic aperitifs are the order of the day, including the eponymous *pastís*, an aniseed spirit that turns white when you add water.

CASA ALMIRALL

Map 2; Carrer de Joaquín Costa, 33, Raval; ///blushed.vase.fishery;
www.casaalmirall.com

This is *the* place to take a date, though you won't be alone; dating app matches are regulars at Casa Almirall. The front section of this 1920s gem is done up in full Art Deco flare, with a gorgeous wooden bar. The back (beyond the dividing screen), meanwhile, is decorated speakeasy-style. Settle on one of the velvet sofas, order a bottle of red and prepare to spend the evening swapping life stories with your date.

» Don't leave without ordering a couple of vermouths, which will come served with soda water.

Shh!

Fancy a sophisticated night in an old members-only smoking club? Seek out Pipa Club *(www. barcelona pipaclub.com)*, now a classy cocktail joint with DJ sets and a cohort of pool players practising their aim. Hidden behind a tiny door in a corner of Plaça Reial, in the Gothic Quarter, it's not easy to find; look for the Pipa Club plaque, ring the buzzer and keep your fingers crossed that someone answers the door.

Cocktail Joints

When they want to mix things up a bit, Barna locals make for the city's punchy cocktail bars. And, handily, the city has plenty of tempting offerings to quench their thirst.

MARLOWE BAR

Map 1; Carrer del Rec, 24, Born; ///hungry.remain.jotting; 717 702 732

Ever wondered what your cocktail of choice says about you? Marlowe Bar is here to answer that question. How? With nothing by way of a menu. Here you'll chat with expert bartenders (if you're shy, this might not be the place for you), who on sussing out your style will tailor a cocktail just for you. Expect delicious concoctions often made using foraged ingredients.

BALIUS

Map 5; Carrer de Pujades, 196, Poblenou; ///decades.tomb.instead; www.baliusbar.com

Formerly an old pharmacy of the same name, Balius is now a retro-cool vermouth and cocktail bar. Residents around the Rambla and Poblenou love this spot for its simple yet flavour-packed cocktails. Take the signature Sambac cocktail, with pisco, jasmine, camomile and citrus, or The Wall, which blends bourbon and mezcal with grapefruit and a touch of cinnamon. Come on a Sunday and sip your chosen tipple to the sounds of live jazz.

BAR BOADAS

Map 2; Carrer dels Tallers, 1, Raval; ///parties.twigs.jiggle; 933 189 592
Welcome to the oldest cocktail joint in the city. Opened in 1933 by a *coctelero* (cocktail waiter) who honed his skills serving up daiquiris in Havana, Boadas remains a bar of high pedigree – just look at the Art Deco decor, smartly suited waiters and celebrity signatures lining the walls. Yes, the bar is located in the heart of grungy Raval but the guests here are dressed to impress. Put on your finest and prepare for an evening of pure sophistication.
>> Don't leave without trying the dry martini, which is infused with sandalwood and bergamot. *Deliciós.*

PESCA SALADA

Map 2; Carrer de la Cera, 32, Raval; ///tipping.invents.hears; 651 148 670
This place was once a neighbourhood salted cod shop (yes, that was a thing) and on entering you'll see that things remain a little fishy. The space is the size of a fisher's hut, scales are fastened to the ceiling, and is that a lamp in the shape of a tin of mackerel? Punters pack in like sardines for a last round of goldfish bowl-sized G&Ts before hitting the clubs. Pesca Salada really does have the locals hook, line and sinker.

DR. STRAVINSKY

Map 1; Carrer dels Mirallers, 5, Born; ///price.enter.escaping;
www.drstravinsky.cat

This cocktail laboratory could be the den of an eccentric doctor turned wizard – just look at all the bubbling beakers and jars of tinctures. The intrigue doesn't stop at the decor. Take the cocktail menu, which is out designed like an old illustration of the galaxy. Planets are labelled with types of flavour (think smoky, sour, fruity) so you can choose your perfect flavour of cocktail. Expect surprising ingredients like feta cheese, sundried tomato and even sea urchin.

COLLAGE

Map 1; Carrer dels Consellers, 4, Born; ///chatted.rent.hoofs;
www.collagecocktailbar.com

Tucked away on a quiet street, Collage is the place to hide away with a potent seasonal cocktail. Founder and bartender Fernando Requena crafts drinks around the time of year, like the autumnal Smashing Pumpkins cocktail: rye whisky, fortified wine and a spiced syrup of roasted pumpkin – the perfect warmer on a chilly night.

TWO SCHMUCKS

Map 2; Carrer de Joaquín Costa, 52, Raval; ///energy.neutron.sending;
www.schmuckordie.com

When globetrotter and cocktail aficionado Moe Aljaff set foot in Barcelona to run a couple of pop-up bars, he was forced to stay by popular demand. He set up Two Schmucks on a shoestring budget, and the bar soon skyrocketed into the World's 50 Best Bars. But things remain down to earth; the list of expletives on the door hints that this is hardly a posh spot. We are in the Raval, after all.

» Don't leave without supping one of the experimental cocktails from the ever-changing drinks list.

BAR PARADISO

Map 1; Carrer de Rera Palau, 4, Born; ///sank.less.between; www.paradiso.cat

Upon arriving at Bar Paradiso, you'll be met by a pastrami shop. Don't fret, you're in the right place. Step inside the shop's fridge (no codewords needed here) and find yourself in a softly lit, mid-century speakeasy with mixologists working their cocktail magic. Genuine magic. We're talking helium-infused coffee clouds perched atop coupes, and tornadoes of pisco, apple kombucha and orange blossom swirling hypnotically at the push of a button. A word to the wise: there are just 12 seats at Bar Paradiso, so get there promptly – else you'll be going home with just a pastrami sandwich.

Try it!
VERMOUTH UNIVERSITY

Don't be late for class at Vermouth University. At Las Vermudas (p61) you'll master a range of cocktail recipes using Barcelona's favourite tipple. Graduating has never been so much fun.

Orxateries and Xocolateries

No coffee, no alcohol – these charming cafés are truly unique to Barcelona. Open all year, **orxateries** *are the go-to in summer, before* **xocolateries** *come into their own in winter.*

DULCINEA
Map 1; Carrer de Petritxol, 2, Gothic Quarter; ///allergy.casual.foods; www.granjadulcinea.com

On sweet-themed Carrer Petritxol – or "chocolate street" – sits this charming *xocolateria* (pronounced *shoo-koo-luh-tuh-REE-uh*). Dulcinea is a blast from the past with its suited waiters and comforting range of traditional (and gloriously gloopy) Catalan chocolate drinks.

SIRVENT
Map 3; Carrer del Parlament, 56, Sant Antoni; ///assures.usual.ranked; www.turronessirvent.com

Ah, Sirvent. This legendary spot is one of Barna's oldest and most beloved *orxateries* (*oor-shuh-tuh-REE-uhs*). These traditional cafés are dedicated to serving the sweetened tiger nut drink *orxata*, a favourite refreshment on the Mediterranean coast, especially in summertime. Hordes of thirsty locals queue up to sit-in with a glass of *orxata* or fill a two-litre container to enjoy at home.

>> Don't leave without pairing your *orxata* with a few *fartons*, which are traditional pastries akin to iced buns.

CAN SOLER

Map 6; Carrer del Mar, 97, Badalona; ///beeline.nimbly.poster; www.artesanssoler.com

When it's feeling hot hot hot, Badalona beachgoers walk just a few steps from the shore to Can Soler for a reviving fix of *orxata*. But the nutty drink isn't the only cooling treat on the menu here; Albert Soler, owner and grandson of the café's founder, has won prizes for his ice cream (no mean feat for a country that loves *gelat*). Orxata or ice cream? It's hot, have both.

GRANJA VIADER

Map 2; Carrer d'en Xuclà, 4, Raval; ///confused.referral.shady; www.granjaviader.cat

This old-world *xocolateria* also happens to be one of the few remaining *granges* (cafés specializing in dairy products) that sprang up across Barcelona in the late 19th century. In fact, the *xocolateria* still has the very marble tables that Picasso sat at to muse and drink, or so they claim. If the balmy summer months make the thought of drinking hot chocolate unbearable, you can enjoy this historic spot with a cold chocolate milk.

XOCOLATERIA LA NENA

Map 4; Carrer de Ramón y Cajal, 36, Gràcia; ///format.fakes.stencil;
www.la-nena-chocolate-cafe.business.site

A hit with Barcelonan families, "The Little Girl" is all bright colours, vintage toys and more than a whiff of chocolate. Afternoons are a little frantic, with parents bringing children in for an after-school treat, so pop by for elevenses and a read of the paper instead, for a more relaxed affair.

EL TÍO CHE

Map 5; Rambla del Poblenou, 44–46, Poblenou; ///fall.input.sprays;
www.eltioche.es

After a morning of sun on Mar Bella beach (p167), and the inevitable sweaty stroll back into the city, a visit to El Tío Che is a must. Sip a glass of *el granziado de cebada* (a malt-based slushy) out on the café terrace and you'll be ready to get back out there before you know it.

PLANELLES DONAT

Map 1; Avinguda del Portal de l'Àngel, 27, Gothic Quarter;
///selects.orange.merchant; www.planellesdonat.com

A beloved institution, Planelles Donat has been in the game since 1929. Silver-haired couples often pop into the old-school *orxateria* for a little treat after mass, sipping heavenly glasses of *orxata* at the café's long marble counter.

» **Don't leave without** calling in at the imposing Cathedral of Barcelona, which pre-dates the Sagrada Família by 400 years.

Liked by the locals

"We started out as a small family business some 20 years ago. We've always wanted to keep the place like a small-café, part of the fabric of the neighbourhood. We don't follow trends: we just do what we do, and do it well. All you need is cocoa and fresh milk!"

PEP CAÑAMERAS,
OWNER OF XOCOLATERIA LA NENA

An evening bar-hopping in
Gràcia's squares

Barna's squares are treated like communal backyards – places to catch up with friends and read the paper. Gràcia locals in particular appreciate their *barri*'s numerous *plaças*, which have retained a charming, villagey feel (Gràcia was a town before it was absorbed into the city in the 1800s). Lined with age-old bodegas and *vermuterias*, these public spaces are ideal for pulling up a chair, enjoying a few tipples and watching the world go by.

1. Bar Virreina
Plaça de la Virreina, 1;
934 153 209
///splash.protect.mainland

2. Bar Canigó
Carrer de Verdi, 2;
www.barcanigo.com
///composed.zoom.waddled

3. Sol Soler
Plaça del Sol, 21;
www.solsoler.barcelona
///tenses.observes.stump

4. Bar Bodega Quimet
Carrer de Vic, 23;
932 184 189
///drivers.sailors.cages

5. Mustà Shawarma
Carrer de Mozart, 4;
935 008 591
///fillers.towers.hops

Plaça del Diamant
///recently.teachers.stretch

Plaça de la Vila de Gràcia
///puns.parrot.candles

1 Begin with a snack at
BAR VIRREINA

Don't let Bar Virreina's laminated menu deter you: these guys do the best *bocadillos* (sandwiches) on Plaça de la Virreina.

In **Plaça del Diamant** *stands a statue of the protagonist from Mercè Rodoreda's novel that took its name from this very square.*

2 Step back in time at
BAR CANIGÓ

Order a vermouth at Bar Canigó. Before the war, the owner's grandfather sold a glass of the good stuff for less than a *peseta*. It's pricier these days, but served just as it was back then.

GRÀCIA

3 Soak up the scene in
SOL SOLER

Order a beer and some *patatas bravas* at Sol Soler and watch buskers perform for the crowds milling about in Plaça del Sol.

Plaça de la Vila de Gràcia *is home to the barri's emblematic clock tower and has been the setting of everything from revolts to weddings.*

5 Finish up at
MUSTÀ SHAWARMA

End the night at this family-run Syrian spot, famed for its shawarma with spicy-as-hell hot sauce.

4 Raise a glass at
BAR BODEGA QUIMET

Run by two brothers, Bar Bodega Quimet serves wine from the barrel. Stop in at this characterful old-timer for a glass of red.

0 metres   200
0 yards   200

SHOP

Eco-conscious fashion, pre-loved vinyl and handmade homeware: you need only glimpse Barna's shopping scene to see that this is a city of movers, shakers and makers.

Vintage Gems

Barna has been setting trends for decades. Today young fashionistas pay homage to those who came before them by adding vintage pieces to their wardrobes. Here are some of their favourite shops.

COTTON VINTAGE

Map 4; Carrer d'Enric Granados, 26, Eixample; ///paints.ever.copycat; www.cottonvintage.es

Shopping vintage needn't involve rummaging through piles of old Hawaiian shirts and moth-eaten cardigans. Take Cotton Vintage, where stock – think Dior sunglasses, Manolos and Versace coats – is neatly arranged throughout. It's all thanks to the team of Carrie Bradshaw-esque collectors, who know the story behind every luxury item. High-end fashion without hurting the planet? Yes, please.

HUMANA VINTAGE

Map 1; Avinguda de Francesc Cambó, 30–36, Born; ///cubes.answer.drilled; www.humana-spain.org

Spain's main chain of charity shops, Humana stocks run-of-the-mill clothing donated by those enjoying a good clear-out. Staff at Humana Vintagecarefully select and display the most striking donations,

Humana stores run regular sales, with items going for as little as €1. Check social media for dates.

appealing to Barna's famously stylish locals. Vintage shell suit? Oh yes. Jazzy shirts? Of course. Leather briefcases? Look no further.

L'ARCA

Map 1; Carrer dels Banys Nous, 20, Gothic Quarter; ///late.files.diggers; www.larcabarcelona.com

The grande dame of Barcelona's vintage scene, L'Arca is more atelier than second-hand store. A team of specialist seamstresses have been restoring and reworking delicate fabrics here since 1980. Ever swooned over Kate Winslet's wardrobe in *Titanic*? Well, a lot of her gowns were restored at this stunningly curated boutique. Lovers of old-world glamour are regulars here, fingering the antique kimonos, Manila shawls and flowing linen dresses.

» Don't leave without checking out the selection of wedding dresses; there are some truly elegant gowns here, at wallet-friendly prices.

PETITS ENCANTS

Map 5; Carrer de les Basses de Sant Pere, 24, Born; ///bumps.switched.gave; 933 193 151

Looking to refurbish your flat? Petits Encants is here for you. Crammed with one-of-a-kind treasures and antiques, like wrought-iron streetlamps, gilded grandfather clocks and mahogany sea chests, this relic harks back to the Barcelona of the history books. In essence, Zara Home has got nothing on this cave of wonders.

MERCAT DELS ENCANTS

Map 5; Avinguda Meridiana, 63, Poble Nou; ///preoccupied.sailed.glitz;
www.encantsbarcelona.com

Built to organize the unwieldy flea market that once took place nearby,
there's still no containing the jumble sale that is Mercat dels Encants.
Inside, a basement space is full of rummage-ready treasures waiting
to be discovered, while the top floor is home to less-hectic market stalls.

HOLALA! PLAÇA

Map 2; Carrer de Valldonzella, 2, Raval; ///thuds.mushroom.pastels;
www.holala-ibiza.com

Whichever area of Barna you're in, chances are you'll mingle with
locals kitted out in pre-loved fashion from Holala! Plaça. The team
here have been handpicking pieces from flea markets since 1972. Pop
into the store for a browse and, an hour later, you'll stumble out with a
dapper trouser suit – and a fetching leather suitcase to take it home in.

LA PRINCIPAL RETRO & CO

Map 2; Carrer de Ferlandina, 37, Raval; ///trendy.circular.crowbar;
www.laprincipalretro.com

Everyone knows it: the 1990s are back. La Principal Retro & Co
stocks original 90s pieces that will make you feel truly nostalgic:
snazzy tracksuits, flashy designer jeans, oversized bomber jackets.
It's like the Spice Girls are top of the charts again.

» Don't leave without following Barna's hipsters by picking up one
of the store's totes, inspired by Russian posters for the 1992 Olympics.

FLAMINGOS VINTAGE KILO

Map 2; Carrer dels Tallers, 31, Raval; ///submit.remains.caravan;
www.vintagekilo.com

North American fashion is the name of the game at vintage empire
Flamingos, which bursts at the seams with pieces sourced in Texas,
NYC and Los Angeles. It's this branch that keeps Barna's students
coming back again and again, thanks to the best selection of 80s
sports gear, 90s sweaters and vintage Vans – all on sale by the kilo.

LULLABY VINTAGE

Map 2; Carrer de la Riera Baixa, 22, Raval; ///changes.hunter.stunner;
934 430 802

The crowning jewel of vintage hotspot Carrer de la Riera Baixa,
Lullaby Vintage attracts eagle-eyed magpies with glittering displays of
costume jewellery from bygone eras. If you can, come on a Saturday
afternoon when the street transforms into an alfresco vintage market.

Keep an eye on Two Market's
website *(www.marketsbarcelona.*
com), where a range of vintage
sales are announced each
week. The markets are usually
held in spaces throughout
Sant Andreu and Poble Nou
and, yes, some of them might
involve a bit of a schlep. But,
with bargains to be found at
the regular €1 markets and
kilo sales, it's more than worth
the extra 10 minutes spent
getting there.

Book Nooks

Catalans love books so much that on 23 April – the day of Catalunya's patron saint (Sant Jordi) – they exchange books and roses. This adoration for the written word translates to Barna's bookshop scene.

LAIE CCCB

Map 2; Plaça dels Àngels, 1, Raval; ///cutaway.unrealistic.frost; www.laie.es

After exploring the CCCB *(p129)* – one of the city's most important cultural centres – art and design students quench their creative thirst at the centre's bookshop. Laie CCCB lives up to its privileged location, with gorgeous coffee table books dedicated to art, cinema and cultural theory arranged oh-so artfully (almost too pretty to touch, in fact).

ALTAÏR

Map 4; Gran Via de les Corts Catalanes, 616, Eixample; ///heeding.poet.hamper; www.altair.es

You're holding this book in your hands so we reckon you're a fellow traveller. Sate your wanderlust at Altaïr, Barcelona's specialist travel book emporium. Spread across two floors, and decorated with globes and suitcases, here you'll discover travel writing for every

Altaïr has a message board where you can post info about a trip you're planning to find a travel buddy.

destination under the sun. Pick up a guidebook and start planning your next getaway in the basement café – we'll see you there.

LA RAPOSA

Map 3; Carrer de Tapioles, 47, Poble Sec; ///divide.rinses.above; www.laraposacoop.org

This one is so much more than just a bookshop – it's a community. Founded by three friends, Moma, Alba and Nat, cooperative La Raposa is a social space for sharing feminist and queer ideas. Naturally it's also one of the best stores in Barcelona to pick up a book on these subjects. After buying a tome or two, grab a drink at the shop's café; you'll find yourself in deep discussion with local activists, intellectuals and plucky rebels before you know it.

» Don't leave without tucking into the vegan set menu out in La Raposa's garden – the perfect fuel to start your new book.

LA CENTRAL

Map 4; Carrer de Mallorca, 237, Eixample; ///nests.enforced.farm; www.lacentral.com

Shadow of the Wind fans: there's something Cemetery-of-Forgotten-Books-like about La Central, with its endless wooden bookcases and creaking floorboards. But the real magic lies in the store's gorgeous stone-walled and fairy-lit patio garden – the ideal place to get lost in a book.

MARCAPÁGINAS

Map 3; Carrer de Llançà, 32, Eixample; ///empty.posts.surveyed;
www.libreriamarcapáginas.com

Learning Catalan? Consider brushing up with a graphic novel (a
picture says a thousand words, after all). Tucked away behind Plaça
Espanya, this temple to the graphic novel is the best place to pick
up a read that won't have you reaching for an online translator.

LATA PEINADA

Map 2; Carrer de la Verge, 10, Raval; ///starters.motel.tides;
www.latapeinada.com

Barcelona has been the publishing capital of the Hispanosphere
for a century, and this bookshop celebrates the fact. Lovers of all
things Latin American are regulars at Lata Peinada's book events,
workshops, concerts and annual LatAm literature festival.

Shh!

The University of Barcelona
is found right in the city centre,
a setting that reflects education
being at the very heart of
Catalan identity. But few visitors
realise that its university library
is also open to them. Enter and
you'll find literature students
nose-deep in books, maths
students jabbing feverishly at
calculators and shelves of tomes
that have survived centuries.
Take it all in before heading to
the lovely gardens, where you'll
make friends with the countless
cats who call them home.

HIBERNIAN

Map 4; Carrer del Montseny, 17, Gràcia; ///school.purest.sounds;
www.hibernianbooks.com

If you're the kind of reader who covets the smell of an old book, look
no further: you've found nirvana. Second-hand bookshop Hibernian
specializes in English-language books, with many going for under €5;
trade in an old novel and the lovely staff will even give you a discount.
» Don't leave without taking your purchase over to Plaça de la
Revolució to enjoy the book and square in their full glory.

ODD KIOSK

Map 4; Carrer de València 222, Eixample; ///salutes.cable.paddle;
www.libreriacomplices.com

With the rise of digital media, Barcelona's newsstands needed
some fresh life breathed into them – and that's exactly what Odd
Kiosk does. The dinky little street stall is fast becoming a favourite
spot among the city's LGBTQ+ community, with its carefully curated
range of queer books, magazines, prints and zines.

FINESTRES

Map 4; Carrer de la Diputació, 249, Eixample; ///strut.communal.jolly;
www.llibreriafinestres.com

New kid on the block Finestres opened in 2021 as a place to read
books, not just buy them. Plush sofas pepper the stylish store, tempting
locals to kick back with a paperback. Those inspired by their reads can
head to the patio garden for a chat (it's a strictly quiet space inside).

Home Touches

Barcelonans are a stylish bunch and this doesn't stop at their wardrobes. Locally woven baskets, artisanal ceramics and hand-poured candles make a home here. And you can buy a bit of Barna to take home, too.

BON VENT

Map 1; Carrer de l'Argenteria, 41, Born; ///costumes.regime.saga; www.bonvent.cat

It doesn't get more Mediterranean than Bon Vent, a concept store that has all the vibes of a chic villa on Spain's southern coast. Artisanal wares include pretty glassware, wicker baskets and hand-painted tiles. Perfect pieces for bringing a little gust of fresh sea air into your city flat.

RAIMA

Map 1; Carrer Comtal, 27, Gothic Quarter; ///deny.weeks.petition; www.raima.cat

Home workers wanting to beautify their office space can't resist Raima. The six-storey stationery Shangri-la stocks 3,000 types of paper (who knew there were so many?), plus colour-coded displays of notebooks, fancy fountain pens and classy desk planners – everything needed to make your home office a bit more cheerful.

ESPARTERIA LLUCH

Map 3; Gran Via de les Corts Catalanes, 339, Sants;
///reserved.gloves.dribble; www.esparterialluch.wordpress.com

A far cry from the pricey design stores that self-proclaimed style mavens go weak at the knees for, this cavern is now the city's last remaining handmade wicker and woven *esparto* grass specialist. You could spend hours here, rummaging through the teetering stacks to get your hands on that perfect wicker fruit bowl or picnic basket.

» Don't leave without learning more about local design at nearby Poble Espanyol, Barcelona's open-air architectural museum.

GREY STREET

Map 2; Calle Jovellanos, 1, Raval; ///waitress.parrot.monkey;
www.greystreetbarcelona.com

With a bit of everything, Grey Street is just the place for sniffing out a gift, especially when you don't know where to begin. Everything this quirky concept store stocks – ceramics, planters, tea towels – is artsy and within your budget. Rest assured you won't leave empty-handed.

Try it!
PHOTOGRAPHY ART

Prefer to hang your own artwork on the wall? Head to Lomography in Born to learn camera basics and printing techniques, or attend a street photography session *(www.microsites.lomography.com)*.

RIBES & CASALS

Map 4; Roger de Llúria, 7, Eixample; ///fortress.intervals.hardens;
www.ribescasals.com

There's no better way to look the part in this style-conscious capital than by sporting a striped Ribes & Casals tote bag. And your home deserves to look the part as much as you, right? At Barna's go-to fabric emporium, locals source materials for everything from a new cushion to a pair of curtains. Not so crafty yourself? Just pick up a ready-made home furnishing (and a tote, of course).

FANTASTIK

Map 5; Carrer de Joaquín Costa, 62, Raval; ///speakers.proper.those;
www.fantastik.es

This small homeware hotspot in Raval has been brightening up living rooms since 2005. Every surface brims with colourful items sourced from all over the world – between Mexican tablecloths and Indian mirrors, you'll be spoilt for choice for how to brighten up your own.

CERERIA ABELLA

Map 2; Carrer de Sant Antoni Abat, 9, Raval; ///darting.nodded.supper;
www.candles.barcelona

Looking for a little piece of history to take home? It was 1862 when, following the death of her father, Francesca Abella left her village in the Pyrenees for Barcelona. Here she opened a candle shop to serve the homes and churches (her main client) of Raval. The charismatic entrepreneur lit the way for her niece, María Abella, to oversee the business during the Civil War. Today, over a century later, the shop remains in the family and is still going strong, with droves of devoted locals stocking up on scented candles of all colours, shapes and sizes. Francesca would be proud.

GANIVETERIA ROCA

Map 1; Plaça del Pi, 3, Gothic Quarter; ///hamster.forecast.field; www.ganiveteriaroca.com

Aspiring chefs: here's one for you. This knife emporium (*ganivet* means knife in Catalan) has kept Barcelonans' kitchen drawers well-stocked since 1911. You'll find every kind of sharp implement here: chopping knives, Japanese *sashimi* knives, kitchen gadgets, plus pocket knives, scissors, shaving kits — the list goes on. Extra points for also having the most incredible window display in the city.

» **Don't leave without** a pair of the housebrand multi-use kitchen shears. They're truly cutting-edge (ahem), and will remind you of Barcelona with every snip of butcher's twine or pop of a bottle top.

HEY SHOP

Map 2; Carrer del Dr Dou, 4, Raval; ///garden.lure.swept; www.heyshop.es

You'll likely spot locals sporting Hey tote bags as they go about their lives — the graphic branding is instantly recognizable, thanks to its colourful, typographic design. Stop by the bricks-and-mortar shop to grab one for yourself, or peruse the posters and prints emblazoned with colourful, geometric lettering.

Record Shops

In a city where club nights segue into morning raves, and summer festival weekends are spent dancing in the sun, record shops are holy ground. Here locals rifle through vinyl for their favourite DJ's latest sounds.

BARCELONA CITY RECORDS

Map 5; Jerusalem, 32, Gothic Quarter; ///smoking.breeding.dolphin; www.barcelonacityrecords.com

Locals know that they're in safe hands at Barcelona City Records, famous for its vinyl-only club nights. This airy spot specializes in pre-loved disco, soul, funk and Latin albums from the 60s and 70s. Deep disco addicts are repeat customers, sniffing out hard-to-find albums that will make their vinyl-obsessed friends green with envy.

DISCOS PARADISO

Map 2; Carrer de Ferlandina, 39, Raval; ///climate.smug.logged; www.discosparadiso.com

There's no getting away from it: 20- and 30-something Barcelonans are all about electronic music. When payday arrives, they converge at this music powerhouse, rubbing shoulders with DJs playing at Razzmatazz *(p144)* or Primavera Sound. Everyone rifles dexterously through the crates of new and second-hand records, their eyes darting over house, techno, jungle and synthpop vinyl. Having selected a record, music aficionados take advantage of the store's listening deck to try before they buy – though most know they're guaranteed a banger whatever they've picked up.

ULTRA-LOCAL RECORDS

Map 5; Carrer de Pujades, 113, Poblenou; ///cities.elevate.fairy;
www.ultralocalrecords.blogspot.com

It's all about celebrating Catalan artists and Barcelona-based labels at Ultra-Local. And who knew there were so many? Under the cheery bunting strung across the ceiling, row upon row of crates are stuffed-full with regional albums, LPs and EPs. A record that transports you back to Barna? There's no better souvenir than that.

» Don't leave without showing your support to local artists by sticking around for a live promotional performance.

TVINYL

Map 2; Carrer de Valldonzella, 25, Raval; ///dabble.unit.couple;
www.tvinyl.myshopify.com

With over 30 years' experience in the music business, Jerome "Tvinyl" Dessolier has made it his mission to spread love and music at his shop in Raval. He's a force of nature; give him the lowdown on your music preferences and he'll scour his store to unearth new sounds just for you (house, garage, disco, techno – he knows it all). Bulldog Lola will also likely come and say hello.

REVÓLVER RECORDS
Map 2; Carrer dels Tallers, 11, Raval; ///props.kitchen.insiders;
www.revolverrecords.es

Yellowing gig posters plastered across the walls, peeling black paint and a larger-than-life mural of 70s rockstars KISS: Revólver Records has all the trimmings of an old-school record store. But it's not just the stomping ground of old rockers; the store's extensive collection of electronic, goth and punk attracts young musos too.

» Don't leave without popping next door to sister store Discos Revólver for indie favourites.

JAZZ MESSENGERS
Map 4; Carrer de Còrsega, 202, Eixample; ///trumpet.coughed.into;
www.jazzmessengers.com

Thanks to its semi-basement location and smooth soundtrack, Barna's go-to for jazz and soul could have been plucked from the streets of NYC. Like in any good speakeasy, the staff are only too happy to make your visit extra special by dishing out recommendations, including music-themed books to pair with your vinyl.

ESPAI SALVADISCOS
Map 3; Plaça de Santa Madrona, 4, Poble Sec; ///muddle.vocally.ranks;
www.salvadiscos.co

The name here literally translates as "album saver", which explains the lifebuoy hanging incongruously in the middle of the shop. The passionate team at Salvadiscos save unwanted records from the attics and cellars of spring-cleaning grandparents and from boxes of junk thrown out on the street (sacrilege, we know). Given the store's unorthodox methods of sourcing music, Barcelona's vinyl junkies hit up this chocolate box of curiosities safe in the knowledge there's always something unique on offer.

EL GENIO EQUIVOCADO

Map 4; Carrer de Benet Mercadé, 22, Gràcia; ///points.totally.february; www.egebotiga.com

We can think of worse ways to spend an hour or two than in the company of DJs Pin&Pon – Joan and Rafa to their friends – at El Genio Equivocado. With their own record label of the same name, the duo kit out this stylish shop with indie records, cassettes and CDs (all old and new), plus books on music and queer culture, and branded merch. Best of all? The partners in life, music and business host vermouth-fuelled live music events here in store.

Don't miss shopping arcade Galeries Olímpia, in Sant Antoni *(Ronda de Sant Pau, 17)*, where you'll discover four little-known second-hand record stores: Glove Records Shop, Vinilarium, Crokan's Mutant Store and Rhythm Control. They're tiny but the best things come in small packages, right? All four stores open at 3pm and, handily, the arcade bar opens at 5pm. Happy digging!

Indie Clothing Stores

Yes, Barcelona is one of the world's fashion capitals but the city is also making waves with its independently owned fashion stores and eco-conscious clothing lines. Feel-good fashion with a heart? Count us in.

ANGLE STORE

Map 1; Carrer dels Mirallers, 10, Born; ///cobras.sticky.pads;
www.anglestore.com

In the fight against fast fashion, Angle Store creates clothing that is both timeless in style and long-lasting in quality. An architect by trade, store owner and designer Claudia Roca applies the principles of modular design to clothing, creating practical and easy-to-match pieces in minimalist shapes and colours.

AVEC STUDIO

Map 6; Carrer de Calaf, 25, Sarrià-Sant Gervasi; ///vest.tablets.exhales;
www.avec-studio.com

Leading the way in the slow-fashion scene, Avec Studio's Inés and Alejandro are all about making clothes ethically and responsibly. Everything is solely designed and produced here in Barna, so you can expect great craftsmanship and no air miles.

BLAW STORE

Map 5; Carrer del Bruc, 22, Eixample; ///dome.slogged.about;
www.blawstore.com

Self-proclaimed "House of Men" BLAW Store is dedicated to curating every aspect of a man's life (food, hygiene, home decor, fashion: you name it, they've got it). Its house labels offer understated, quality basics at good prices, which sit alongside in-demand names like Deus, Denham and Patagonia.

BRAVA FABRICS

Map 3; Carrer del Parlament, 21, Sant Antoni; ///awkward.curbed.paints;
www.bravafabrics.com

Imagine all the tropes of hipster life: avocados, vermouth, coffee. Brava Fabrics has embraced these motifs across its shirt patterns, because why be ashamed of things we like? Catering to both men and women, Brava is committed to using eco-friendly materials, too.

» Don't leave without making like a hipster and ordering a flat white at Sant Antoni's Federal Café *(p69)*, just down the road.

LASER

Map 2; Carrer del Dr Dou, 2, Raval; ///tags.basic.stumps;
www.laser-bcn.com

Laser pays homage to its home – a hub of culture, art and diversity – by collaborating with street artists and illustrators to create the "Rawal Artists" collection. The dedicated team controls the whole process, from designing to distributing clothing, no middlemen in sight.

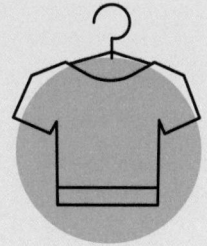

Liked by the locals

"I always dreamed of studying design in Barcelona and presenting at fashion week – to be part of the Barcelona fashion scene. It's a city where creativity and the fashion industry have always worked hand-in-hand, where you can find high-end brands alongside stores run by young designers."

RUBÉN GÓMEZ, JEWELLERY DESIGNER

TOPMANTA

Map 2; Carrer d'en Roig, 13, Raval; ///driver.supplier.timeless;
www.manteros.org

You'll likely notice the sale of sunglasses and accessories on the city's pavements; this is the *topmanta* trade, largely driven by undocumented migrants from the African diaspora. In recent years, the *manteros* (street sellers) established a syndicate to protect their rights. Before they knew it, they'd set up this store in Raval, showcasing the locally made collection "Legal Clothing, Illegal People". Locals are chuffed to see it, as all profits go towards anti-racism causes.

SSSTUFFF

Map 5; Carrer del Duc, 7, Gothic Quarter; ///upwards.backlog.tapers;
www.ssstufff.com

Intentionally disguised as a cornershop, this kooky concept store pushes the limits of fashion design. Among the out-there items are clothes made to be ripped and throw-back scratch-'n'-sniff tops. Feeling those 90s vibes? You'll fit right at home here.

PITAGORA

Map 5; Carrer de Llull, 27, Poblenou; ///deflect.effort.logs; www.pitagora.es

Talk to any Barcelonan and they'll tell you that Poblenou is Barna's design district. And it's here you'll find clothing shop Pitagora. This spot has dropped the constructs of gender and designed all its clothes to fit and suit anybody and everybody, with simple designs and natural colours.

Gourmet Treats

Barcelona is a foodie's paradise and it doesn't stop at restaurants. Around every corner you'll find tempting artisan food shops and markets, ripe with edible treats just waiting to be devoured.

VILA VINITECA "LA TECA"

Map 1; Carrer dels Agullers, 9, Born; ///spotty.prance.invite; www.vilaviniteca.es

Facing sister wine shop Vila Viniteca, gourmet grocer "La Teca" is the ultimate place to stock up ahead of a dinner party. Fill your basket with cured meats, canned seafoods and premium cheeses (there are 300 to choose from). It's not cheap but your guests will thank you.

Shh!

Not sure what wine to serve to your friends with dinner? Learn from the best at a private wine tasting at "La Teca". In the grocer's gorgeous 15th-century stone cellar you'll sample various wines plus food products to go alongside them, all with the advice and expertise of the store's staff. You'll be wowing your friends in no time.

LA BOQUERIA

**Map 2; La Rambla, 91, Raval; ///mushroom.promotes.perkily;
www.boqueria.barcelona**

Barcelonans joke that if you can't find an ingredient at La Boqueria then you need to change your recipe. Early in the morning, before the throngs of *guiris* (tourists) arrive, they descend on the city's most famous food market, armed with their shopping lists and canvas shopping bags. They enter via the back and side entrances (the front entrance is used by *guiris*), knowing that it's in these hidden corners that they'll find the market's finest wild mushrooms, *jamón*, wheels of cheese and tins of saffron.

>> **Don't leave without** stopping for lunch at the legendary El Quim de la Boqueria. Up at the restaurant's counter, you'll tuck into traditional tapas, all made from ingredients sourced here in the market.

MERCAT DE SANTA CATERINA

**Map 1; Avinguda de Francesc Cambó, 16, Santa Caterina;
///decrease.propose.belts; www.mercatdesantacaterina.com**

Barcelona's second most famous food market, Mercat de Santa Caterina stands on the site of the medieval Convent of Saint Catherine (you'll find the archaeological site at the back of the market). The food hall has long kept city workers well-fed, first in the 19th century, when the market building was constructed, and now in the 21st. Museum staff and local professionals weave through the stalls and vendors on their lunch breaks, eyeing up the kaleidoscopic displays of fruit, buckets of olives and dishes of paella – just like those who came before them.

LA BOTIFARRERIA DE SANTA MARIA

Map 1; Carrer de Santa Maria, 4, Born; ///command.credit.proceeds;
www.labotifarreria.com

Pork is king here in Barcelona; insist a meat-eating local names their favourite type and they'll say *botifarra* (a white sausage and Catalan speciality). This beloved *botifarreria* in Born has one of the most varied assortments of house-made *botifarras* in the city. Choose from a range of ready-to-grill sausages, stuffed with tasty morsels like dates, gruyère or stewed cuttlefish – great on the go or for a dinnertime treat.

» Don't leave without buying a few cooked sausages prepared with black truffle – the perfect addition to an alfresco feast.

LA CHINATA

Map 1; Passeig del Born, 11, Born; ///acute.units.shelter; www.lachinata.es

Never underestimate the power of the humble olive – gourmet and cosmetics shop La Chinata certainly doesn't. The small chain store is a hotspot for initiated regulars, who come to stockpile olive oils and spreads before topping up their toiletry bags with olive oil soaps, bath gels and room sprays.

XOCOLATES FARGAS

Map 1; Carrer del Pi, 16, Gothic Quarter; ///sometime.early.token;
www.xocolatesfargas.cat

Confectioner Fargas has been charming the masses with its stone-ground chocolate since 1827 and you can still see its 200-year-old mill in action today. Treat yourself to a trademark bar of chocolate

 Visit the Chocolate Museum for more cocoa joy. Tickets even come wrapped around a chocolate bar.

and, for your pals back home, buy some bags of *Catanies*, a Catalan sweet made from roasted marcona almonds set inside balls of white chocolate praline.

ENTRE LATAS

Map 4; Carrer de Torrijos, 16, Gràcia; ///pizza.holdings.civil;
www.entrelatas-bcn.com

If there's one staple foodstuff you'll find in every Catalan kitchen, it's gourmet tinned food, or *conserves*. We're talking canned fish, pâtés, vegetables – basically anything that pairs with a beer or vermouth. Entre Latas owner Paola Fornasaro is a graphic designer turned foodie hero and prides herself on curating tempting and beautifully packaged *conserves* that won't stay in your cupboard for long. Easily packable, and pretty to boot, these are the perfect Barcelonan goodies to take home.

CASA CAROT

Map 1; Carrer de la Dagueria, 16, Gothic Quarter;
///finally.games.repeats; 606 739 093

When Barcelonans are buying provisions for a sun-drenched picnic in Parc de la Ciutadella *(p176)*, they call in at this conveniently (read: lethally) placed artisan cheese shop. Casa Carot prides itself on small-production Catalan cheeses, all made from well-treated animals – producers are often found in store giving talks and tastings (check social media for dates).

Rest your feet at
GRASSHOPPER
RAMEN BAR

Recharge with a tasty bowl of ramen and locally brewed craft beer at Grasshopper.

4

PLAÇA DE
LA LLANA

Update your look at
OSCAR H GRAND

Clothing designer Oscar is all about creative freedom, quality and elegance. Visit his workshop and store and try on some of his gorgeous jackets and overshirts.

PLAÇA DE
JAUME
SABARTÉS

CARRER DEL POU
DE LA CADENA

LA PRINCESA

CARRER DE

CARRER DE LA BARRA DE FERRO

CARRER DE MONTCADA

5

CARRER

CARRER DELS COTONERS

BORN

CARRER DELS
VIGATANS

CARRER DELS BANYS VELLS

Get creative at
TERRA I PELL

Feeling inspired? Join a ceramics, jewellery or leather-making class with tutors Puri and Victor at their arts studio.

6

CARRER DELS

SOMBRERERS

3

Browse for treats at
CASA GISPERT

This old-fashioned shop hasn't changed much since 1851. Stock up on gourmet treats and locally roasted coffees.

Support local design at
IVORI

Discover young Barcelonan designers at Ivori, a clothing store that takes a chance on local talent with a curated selection of garments.

2 CARRER DELS MIRALLERS

Born's streets are named after items crafted here in the 15th and 16th centuries, like Carrer dels Mirallers – the street of mirrors.

PLAÇA
DE SANTA
MARIA

VIA
LAIETANA

PLAÇA DE
VÍCTOR
BALAGUER

0 metres   50

0 yards   50

An afternoon of
artisan shopping

Early inhabitants of Born (one of the oldest *barris* in Barcelona) were fishers and labourers but, as time passed, noblemen and wealthy merchants settled here. With them grew an appetite for craftsmanship, and so skilled makers seized the opportunity to set-up shop here. Fast forward to today and these medieval streets remain the domain of local artisans and indie boutiques.

1. Alexis Fasoli
Carrer de la Volta dels Tamborets, 4;
www.alexisfasoli.com
///walking.sake.friction

2. Ivori
Carrer dels Mirallers, 7;
www.ivoribarcelona.com
///beams.puffed.overhaul

3. Casa Gispert
Carrer dels Sombrerers 23;
www.casagispert.com/en/
///rush.name.prongs

4. Grasshopper Ramen Bar
Plaça de la Llana, 9;
930 178 484

///cashew.swan.audio

5. Oscar H Grand
Carrer de la Barra de Ferro, 7;
www.oscarhgrand.com
///cherub.restless.reboot

6. Terra i Pell
Carrer dels Banys Vells, 17;
https://terraipell.com
///runners.ended.bumping

Passeig del Born
///steroids.almost.wink

Carrer dels Mirallers
///others.nuanceworked

PLAÇA
COMERCIAL

*Before it thronged with shoppers, **Passeig del Born** was the execution ground for victims of the 15th-century Spanish Inquisition.*

PASSEIG
DEL BORN

CARRER DE L'ESPARTERIA

Visit the workshop of ALEXIS FASOLI

Pop by Alexis Fasoli's atelier boutique to see how he creates leather accessories by hand, using traditional techniques.

PLA DE
PALAU

ARTS & CULTURE

Catalunya's cosmopolitan capital swells with creativity. This is a city built on international aspirations and local inclinations, where old and new live side by side.

City History

If you want to better understand Catalan pride, you need only look to the history of its capital. Barcelona has known tragedy, but from the ashes of war and oppression it's risen triumphant.

NATIONAL LIBRARY OF CATALUNYA

Map 2; Carrer de l'Hospital, 56, Raval; ///trades.daunting.clock; www.bnc.cat

If there's an impressive building in Barcelona that you don't know the name of, chances are it's a library. This is a nation of bibliophiles, after all, and Barna locals have 60 public libraries to choose from. Their favourite? The National Library, of course. This literary temple occupies the beautiful 15th- to 18th-century buildings of the Old Hospital de la Santa Creu, where Gaudí died in 1926.

BARCELONA CIVIL WAR TOUR

Map 4; Plaça de Catalunya, Eixample; ///danger.pelting.tunnel; www.thespanishcivilwar.com

Spain strangely doesn't have a permanent museum space dedicated to the Civil War, in spite of cities such as Barcelona bearing its scars. It makes sense, then, to book a walking tour with historian Nick Lloyd,

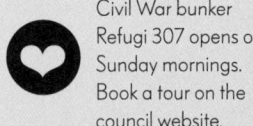 Civil War bunker Refugi 307 opens on Sunday mornings. Book a tour on the council website.

who knows all there is to know about the Second Spanish Republic and the arrival of the Franco regime. Prefer to go it alone? Turn to page 136 for a condensed tour.

CASTELL DE MONTJUÏC

Map 3; Carretera de Montjuïc, 66, Montjuïc; ///bikers.proud.locate;
www.barcelona.cat/castelldemontjuic

Built by Catalan loyalists, this 17th-century fortress has seen countless revolts and wars, especially in the region's fight for independence. Today, families hosting out-of-town friends traipse around the castle grounds and exhibits, learning about the anarchists who met their fate in the castle's chilling dungeons.

» Don't leave without continuing on to Montjuïc Cemetery. It's a beautiful spot and its views are second to none.

MONESTIR DE PEDRALBES

Map 6; Baixada del Monestir 9, Pedralbes; ///followers.army.vivid;
www.monestirpedralbes.barcelona

Churches dot every street corner in Barna, prompting folk to pray between running errands and cooking lunch. These holy spaces are as much a part of the buzzing city as tapas bars and art museums. But Pedralbes Monastery is special. Hidden away from the modern city, the monastery preserves its heavenly feeling of peace and calm. Make a pilgrimage here and the only sounds you'll hear in the 14th-century cloisters are the bubbling of fountains and the singing of resident nuns.

MUHBA EL CALL

Map 1; Placeta de Manuel Ribé, 3, Gothic Quarter; ///response.diner.regard;
www. barcelona.cat/museuhistoria/en/muhba-el-call

Before the Spanish Inquisition, when Catholic monarchs sought to
convert those of other faiths (often by torture), a thriving Jewish
community lived in a patch of the Gothic Quarter (called El Call).
This dimly lit 13th-century house gives a fascinating insight into their
lives and lasting influence on the city.

EL BORN CENTRE DE CULTURA I MEMÒRIA

Map 1; Plaça Comercia,l 12, Born; ///upcoming.puppy.talents;
www.elbornculturaimemoria.barcelona.cat

Parents trying to instil some Catalan spirit in their kids are regulars
at this cultural centre. We say centre, it's more of an archaeological
site. In 1994, renovation of the old central market was put on hold

Shh!

Under Franco, the former men's
prison Carcel La Model was
once crowded with political
prisoners and anti-fascists,
as well as gay men and trans
women. The site hasn't been in
use as a prison since 2017, which
is why it's now possible for visitors
to remember these injustices by
paying a visit. Currently, tours
are only available in Catalan
and Spanish, but English tours
are said to be coming *(www.
lamodel.barcelona)*.

when ruins of the old city emerged. Today, information boards tell the story of the 1713–14 War of Succession, in which Barcelona fell to the French and Spanish and this area was razed to the ground. It was then, too, that the Catalan language was banned.

» Don't leave without stopping by Santa Maria del Mar, a rare church built by the city's tradespeople rather than the aristocracy.

GAUDÍ HOUSE MUSEUM

Map 6; Carretera del Carmel, 23, Gràcia; ///divides.sharp.desktop; www.casamuseugaudi.org

Barcelona's architectural heritage runs deep; just look up to see the whimsical *Modernista* style that boomed in the late 19th century. The poster boy for this ground-breaking movement was none other than the renowned architect Antoni Gaudí. Mega fans make for this museum, which was once his house.

MUSEUM OF THE OLYMPICS & SPORT AND OLYMPIC STADIUM

Map 3; Avinguda de l'Estadi, 60, Montjuïc; ///wizards.topping.tall; www.museuolimpicbcn.cat

It was the 1992 Olympics that put Barcelona firmly on the tourist map. Take a deep dive into all this and more at the Museum of the Olympics & Sport before crossing over the road to enter the stadium where the 1992 magic took place. Interesting fact: the stadium was built in 1936 – not in the 1990s – as an anti-fascist protest against the Berlin Olympics.

Modernista Barcelona

*Don't be fooled by the word **Modernista**; Barna's defining architectural style is flouncier than its austere Modernist counterparts. The much-loved Sagrada Família is justifiably famous but other gems lie in wait.*

ELS QUATRE GATS

Map 1; Carrer de Montsió 3, Gothic Quarter; ///miracle.slices.herb; www.4gats.com

Say *hola* to Barcelona's answer to Le Chat Noir in Paris (Els Quatre Gats means "The Four Cats"). This delightful bar was the meeting place for *Modernistes and* creative thinkers in the early 20th century (Picasso held his first exhibition here). Our top tip? Come by in the evening for live piano music with fellow sophisticates.

QUADRAT D'OR

Map 4; Quadrat d'Or, Eixample; ///closet.thudded.truth

Stretching from Carrer d'Aribau to Passeig de Sant Joan, "The Golden Square" is home to the greatest concentration of *Modernista* buildings in Barcelona. As you take a *passeig* (stroll), you'll notice neo-Gothic features, stained-glass and intricate details that define the works of Gaudí and his contemporaries. And if you need a paracetamol after a heavy night in the bars of Raval, many of the quadrant's pharmacies are unexpectedly decadent examples of Catalan *Modernisme* (Farmàcia Aguilar Pérez is especially lovely).

PALAU DE LA MÚSICA CATALANA

Map 1; Carrer del Palau de la Música 4–6, Born; ///chew.tested.beefed; www.palaumusica.cat

Parents in town? The darling of Barcelona's *Modernista* scene is just the ticket. Designed by Barcelona-born Lluís Domènech i Montaner, this music hall was built for the Catalan Choral Society. Today you don't have to be a classical music buff to enjoy the space; concerts cover jazz, flamenco and even pop. That aside, the real star of the show is the breathtaking inverted stained-glass dome ceiling.

HOSPITAL DE LA SANTA CREU I SANT PAU

Map 6; Carrer de Sant Antoni Maria Claret 167, El Guinardó; ///twinge.retiring.paints; www.santpaubarcelona.org

Another masterpiece by Domènech i Montaner, this gorgeous hospital was converted into a museum in 2009. Make a morning of it: digest some architectural and medical history, then sit and soak up the sun – nature's best medicine – among the orange trees.

>> Don't leave without exiting the hospital grounds via Avinguda Gaudí and following the road all the way to the Sagrada Família.

Solo, Pair, Crowd

A day in Barcelona without a slice of *Modernisme* is unthinkable. Whoever you're with, here are a few ways to get a fix.

FLYING SOLO
Working 9 to 5

In Barcelona for business? Book a desk at Casa de les Punxes, a grand *Modernista* house that's now a co-working space with an all-important café. It beats the office.

IN A PAIR
Let the music play

Slip on your Sunday best and treat yourself and a loved one to a swanky performance at Palau de la Música Catalana. An aftershow glass of cava in the foyer bar is a must.

FOR A CROWD
Party in the park

Stock up on picnic goodies from Mercat de Lesseps and make for Parc Güell. With bizarre architecture and glorious gardens, you and your pals are guaranteed a striking spot.

CASA AMATLLER

Map 4; Passeig de Gràcia 41, Eixample; ///arrives.coaster.softest;
www.amatller.org

Often playing second (or third) fiddle to Gaudí's Casa Batlló and
Casa Milà, this Gothic-inspired gem is wonderfully playful in style.
Marvel at its grandeur and decorative flourishes before heading to
the on-site hot chocolate café; Josep Puig i Cadafalch designed the
house for Barcelona's biggest chocolate magnate.

BELLESGUARD

Map 6; Carrer de Bellesguard 20, Sant Gervasi;
///together.report.brochure; www.bellesguardgaudi.com

While tourists flock to *Modernista* big-hitters, those seeking a
moment of reflection head to this lovely Gaudí manor house.
Tucked away on the city limits, the gardens are dotted with the
remains of a medieval castle that Gaudí took inspiration from.
» Don't leave without taking a look around CosmoCaixa while you're
here. The science museum is housed in a red-brick *Modernista* factory.

PALAU GÜELL

Map 2; Carrer Nou de la Rambla 3–5, Raval; ///spark.driveway.small;
www.palauguell.cat

Many have absent-mindedly strolled past this mansion, which isn't
much to look at from the outside. And yet Palau Güell is considered
one of Gaudí's best designs. You need to step inside to see why (look
to the stained-glass windows casting colours across the dark stone).

Art Museums

Picasso, Dalí, Miró – these giants of the art world all once called Barcelona home. The city is still pumping out artists to this day, and its institutions continue to mount masterpieces for the public to swoon over.

MACBA

Map 2; Plaça dels Àngels, 1, Raval; ///cutaway.unrealistic.frost; www.macba.cat

Crowds of beer-swigging skaters and gutterpunks loitering out front, rap battles filling the air on the patio to the side; there's little doubt that MACBA is one of Barcelona's edgier museums. This place is not about pretty paintings of flowers. No: here, the ever-changing exhibits draw the young and curious with topics ranging from architecture to zines, all with a focus on contemporary social issues.

MUSEU PICASSO

Map 1; Carrer de Montcada, 15–23, Born; ///deluded.trumped.tamed; www.museupicasso.bcn.cat

All of the famous Picasso works that you're hoping to see are in museums in other Spanish cities. But it doesn't matter. Here in Barcelona – the artist's one-time home – fans can take a deep

The Picasso Museum is free of charge on Thursday evenings (winter and summer times vary, though). dive into some of his lesser-known creations (we're talking pottery, sketches, metalwork) in one of the most extensive Picasso collections in the world.

MNAC

Map 3; entrance via Avinguda dels Montanyans, Montjuïc;
///sticking.strict.nation; www.museunacional.cat

Let's be honest, contemporary art isn't for everyone. For those who prefer things a little more traditional, the Museu Nacional d'Art de Catalunya (MNAC to its friends) is a great one-stop-shop for all things Catalan art-related. The main event is the Romanesque section, which features entire chapels pulled from early Medieval churches in the Pyrenees.

» Don't leave without wandering round the back to find the Jardí Botànic Històric *(p177)*, a botanical garden built in a disused quarry.

DISSENY HUB

Map 5; Plaça de les Glòries Catalanes, 38, Poblenou;
///diplomat.factories.dolphin; www.dissenyhub.barcelona

Yes, Barcelona has a long history with architecture and the decorative arts but it's not all about fancy houses and ceramic bowls. The Disseny Hub (or "Design Hub") takes visitors on a journey through all aspects of design: propaganda posters, household appliances, fashion. It's diverse and all-encompassing – there's even some design love for the humdrum toilet.

LA VIRREINA CENTRE DE LA IMATGE

Map 2; La Rambla, 99, Raval; ///best.frowns.winks;
www.ajuntament.barcelona.cat/lavirreina

Just off the thronging tourist trap of La Rambla lies this space dedicated to all things photography. Thought-provoking, modern and (wonderfully) free, exhibitions are constantly changing. Previous displays include retrospectives of artists Sophie Calle and Paula Rego; a look at society via portraits of Barcelonans taken across 30 years; and explorations of events in recent history, such as the Arab Spring.

FUNDACIÓ TÀPIES

Map 4; Carrer d'Aragó, 255, Eixample; ///unwell.rainy.fizzle;
www.fundaciotapies.org

Meet local lad Antoni Tàpies, one of Catalunya's most experimental artists of the postwar period. (Don't worry if you've never heard of him, even some locals haven't.) Largely self-taught, he created heavily textured works that were frequently inspired by Catalan culture and language. If you're a fan of all things avant-garde or are just up for something different, it's well worth checking out the rotating exhibitions.

MOCO MUSEUM

Map 1; Carrer de Montcada, 25, Born; ///running.cool.career;
www.mocomuseum.com

Situated in a 16th-century palace once reserved for the elite, fresh-faced Moco (it opened in 2021) is the city's most photogenic gallery, inside and out. The walls are hung with an abundance of contemporary artworks, by the likes of Warhol, Basquiat, Banksy and Dalí. Newer works include Moco's immersive digital installations – such as Studio Irma's *Diamond Matrix*, a Kusama-esque room of mirrors and lights – that will be the envy of all your social media followers.

CAIXAFORUM

Map 3; Avinguda de Francesc Ferrer i Guàrdia, 6–8, Montjuïc;
///treaties.rocks.trains; www.caixaforum.es

By day, families flock to this red-brick *Modernista* factory for a dose of culture; exhibitions here touch on everything from ancient artifacts to video game art, and all have educational spaces to keep little ones engaged. Come evening, the grown-ups take over, enjoying talks, concerts and film screenings in the entrance hall.

FUNDACIÓ JOAN MIRÓ

Map 3; entrance via Avinguda Miramar, Montjuïc;
///prompting.panning.deliver; www.fmirobcn.org

Art buffs and students alike come to worship at this shrine to Barcelona-born Joan Miró, one of Catalunya's most famous Surrealist painter and sculptor. The striking concrete museum – a gem in its own right, architecturally speaking – is a great place to get up close and personal with the artist's work, which showcases his bold use of colour and experimental shapes.

» **Don't leave without** taking a stroll to Parc Joan Miró to see the 22-m- (72-ft-) high Miró sculpture *Dona i Ocell.*

Cultural Spaces

Yes, Gaudí and Picasso were talented but culture in Barcelona doesn't stop with them. The city has countless spaces that celebrate cinema, performance art and LGBTQ+ stories. Oh, and puppets.

LA CASA DELS ENTREMESOS

Map 1; Plaça de les Beates, 2, Born; ///testers.drill.referral; www.lacasadelsentremesos.cat

We know, a space dedicated to giant puppets seems odd but *els gegants* are (literally) big in Catalan culture. These 4-m- (13-ft)- tall puppets dance with revellers during the *festes majors* (*barri* festivals usually celebrated in the summer months). Each *barri* has its own pair, some of them centuries old. When the party's over, these curious figures of local folklore are housed at La Casa dels Entremesos.

IDEAL

Map 5; Carrer del Dr Trueta 196, Poblenou; ///helpless.brittle.yarn; www.idealbarcelona.com

Once a cinema, then a TV studio and now a temple to the digital arts, IDEAL is all about immersing visitors in its temporary and truly one-of-a-kind displays. Poblenou's creatives spend hours taking in the centre's wall-to-wall holograms, which celebrate the works of specific artists, such as Gustav Klimt or Frida Kahlo. Elements of the masters' works are projected onto the walls of the centre's vast rooms, immersing goggle-eyed spectators into larger-than-life versions of iconic paintings.

CCCB

Map 2; Carrer de Montalegre 5, Raval; ///answers.singer.booth; www.cccb.org

Ravers raise the roof at the Centre de Cultura Contemporània (CCCB) during the summer months, when the contemporary arts centre hosts performances for Sónar and Primavera Sound music festivals. The rest of the year, this is where the curious-minded get a dose of culture by enjoying exhibitions on everything from bacteria to Björk, and attending talks on things like the power and politics of a face mask.

» Don't leave without making the most of the CCCB's ultra-modern VR experiences. Advance booking is an absolute must.

Try it!
STREET ART TOUR

Murals are tagged and updated every day in Barna. Join the good folk of Street Art Barcelona on a tour to find the art in Raval, Born and Poblenou on that given day (*www.streetartbcn.com*).

CENTRE LGBTI

Map 3; Carrer del Comte Borrell, 22, Sant Antoni;
///shopper.passages.secondly; www.ajuntament.barcelona.cat/lgtbi

In a place where being yourself is celebrated, a city council-run centre that's all about honouring queer culture just makes sense. Art installations and photography exhibitions are small but they pack a punch, spotlighting LGBTQ+ stories from a range of perspectives. It's a great spot to mingle with the community without having to fork out at a bar or shout over a deafening sound system.

ARTS SANTA MÒNICA

Map 2; La Rambla, 7, Raval; ///washed.defends.clubs;
https://artssantamonica.gencat.cat

This building might once have been a Renaissance convent but nothing is sacred here, not since Arts Santa Mònica was set up as an interdisciplinary arts centre in the 1980s. The space is a platform for

Shh!

Looking to find the next big name on the art scene? Then head out for a stroll around the old warehouses of L'Hospitalet. Home to a flourishing gallery scene, here you'll find spaces like airy etHall (www.ethall.net), the expansive Ana Mas Projects (www.anamasprojects. com) and the inconspicuous Galeria Alegria (www. galeriaalegria.es) located around the Santa Eulàlia train tracks.

young, up-and-coming artists with a different take on things. Collective projects blur the lines between art practices, with concerts staging medieval compositions in the style of pop queen Madonna, and performances of feminist texts given through the medium of dance.

» Don't leave without having a drink at the bar lounge, where the centre's podcast is recorded – you might even be approached to feature.

FILMOTECA DE CATALUNYA
Map 2; Plaça de Salvador Seguí, 1, Raval; ///races.juggler.rankings; www.filmoteca.cat

Cinephiles come together at this film archive and cinema, one of the few spots in the city where you can watch films in their original language (many commercial cinemas in Spain show dubbed versions). Film-themed artifacts are laid out in the centre's exhibition rooms, while two screens showcase indie, foreign and classic flicks.

BIBLIOTECA PÚBLICA ARÚS
Map 5; Passeig de Sant Joan, 26, Eixample; ///rail.hails.glides; www.bpa.es

Okay, this one isn't technically a cultural space per se, but it's too beautiful to miss. The legacy of Catalan journalist and playwright Rossend Arús, this gorgeous library houses one of the largest collections of books on Freemasonry in the world. Arús hosted Freemason meetings here in the late 1800s before he left the building and his collection of books to the people of Barcelona. You can't take books out bu you're here to take in the sumptuous grandeur.

Get Crafty

Design-savvy Barcelona is a city of makers, and locals love crafting their own little something to take home. Follow their lead and set your creative juices flowing at these varied crafty experiences.

ART&WINE

Map 4; Carrer de la Mare de Déu dels Desemparats 14, Gràcia; ///staging.spelled.goggles; www.artwine.es

Feeling creatively blocked? Always been scared of picking up a paintbrush and letting your imagination run free? There's one simple solution: wine. Art&Wine runs sessions every evening with professional art teachers, to help you bring out your artistic side and give you a chance to socialize with other creatives, all in the most Barcelonan way possible – over a drink.

KANAY TALLER DE CERÀMICA

Map 5; Carrer del Bruc 5, Born; ///preoccupied.struts.promises; www.studiokanay.com

Ceramics are huge in Barna; pick out any group of 30-somethings and you can guarantee one of them attends a ceramics class. Kanay offers a range of workshops, from one-day courses to mastering the potter's wheel. If you don't feel like doing a Demi Moore and getting your hands all covered in clay, sign-up for a short pottery painting workshop instead.

WOOD BERN CARVINGS

Map 6; Carrer de Felip II 181, Sant Andreu; /// dial.jigging.self; www.woodberncarvings.com

At Wood Bern Carvings, Bernat Mercader offers woodcarving classes for all levels. Here, you can create the ultimate Barcelona souvenir and make your very own wooden version of a *panot*, the iconic Barcelona paving tile with a four-petalled flower. (It'll be a lot easier to carry home than its concrete counterpart would be, too.) If you already know your way around a chisel, there's also an open workshop where you can go to practise your craft.

» Don't leave without calling at nearby Nau Bostik, a former factory now home to many creative businesses and regular vintage markets.

TALLER DE 4 PINTORS

Map 1; Carrer de la Portaferrissa 16, Gothic Quarter; ///fattest.reboot.tape; www.tallerde4pintors.cat

What could be more bohemian than a painting and drawing workshop overlooking the spires of the Gothic Quarter? Run by two professional artists, Nuria and Agustí, these classes will help you hone your art skills whether you're just there for a one-off or you've signed up for a series of lessons. With so much inspiration on hand, it's almost impossible not to improve.

MUCHAFIBRA

Map 6; Carrer d'en Copons 3–5, Gothic Quarter; ///awards.swam.surely;
www.muchafibra.com

MuchaFibra is a one-of-a-kind space in Barcelona: a co-working hub for clothing and fabric specialists. It's run by master designers who also put on a whole host of courses on upcycling, pattern-making and other fashion-related skills.

» Don't leave without strolling around the corner to check out Barcelona's iconic mural made up of photos of couples kissing.

THE ESPADRILLES EXPERIENCE

Map 1; Carrer del Call, 7, Gothic Quarter;
///talker.dripped.quirky; www.espadrillesexperience.com

Love them or loathe them, *espardenyes* (or espadrilles) are cool for the summer and rooted in Catalan folk culture. Dating back to the 14th century, these shoes were worn by the working classes who could afford the *esparto* grass needed to make them. Luis and Kathe at Handmade Barcelona share this heritage at their workshops.

ATUELL CERÀMICA

Map 4; Carrer del Montseny 45, Gràcia; ///faced.stacks.layered;
www.atuell.com

Did we mention that Barcelonans are massively into their pottery classes? Well, Atuell is where they hone their new-found skills. This open workshop comes with wheels and kilns, plus a team on hand to help with any questions. It's perfect if you're already handy with your clay.

Liked by the locals

"When you make your own pair of
espadrilles at Handmade, you
become part of the community of
artisans of Barcelona. Every time
you wear a pair of shoes that
you've made yourself, you
remember your trip even more
vividly. That's the magic of
this experience."

LUIS MORENO, FOUNDER OF HANDMADE BARCELONA
AND THE ESPADRILLES EXPERIENCE

An afternoon of
Civil War history

A bloody war played out in Barcelona's streets less than 100 years ago. From 1936 to 1939, right-wing Nationalists led by Franco rained bombs on the city, bringing Barcelona (and wider Catalunya) to its knees. Decades of Catalan oppression ensued under Franco's regime, ending with his death in 1975. The scars of this dark history continue to shape the region's political landscape today.

1. Palau de la Generalitat de Catalunya
Plaça de Sant Jaume, Gothic Quarter
///transfers.fish.whom

2. Plaça de Sant Felip Neri
Gothic Quarter
///squeezed.scout.swept

3. Caelum
Carrer de la Palla, 8; Gothic Quarter; 933 026 993
///levels.teaspoons.migrate

4. Hotel Continental
La Rambla, 138, Eixample;
www.hotelcontinental.com
///sports.exposing.tolls

5. Plaça de Catalunya
Eixample
///parrot.theme.reshape

6. La Rosa de Foc
Carrer de Joaquín Costa, 34, Raval; 933 177 892
///others.brands.huddle

7. Bar Marsella
Carrer de Sant Pau, 65, Raval
///recoup.gold.warm

Apple store
///ranges.typical.door

GRAN VIA DE LES CORTS CATALANES

CARRER DELS TALLERS

Pop into
LA ROSA DE FOC
Buy a thought-provoking read from this politically minded bookshop, which is run by a trade union.

PLAÇA DE ANGELS

6

CARRER DE JOAQUÍN C

CARRER DE LA RIERA ALTA

PLAÇA DEL PEDRÓ

In 1939, banners of Lenin and Stalin hung across the facade of the Communist Party HQ, a building that now houses the **Apple store**.

PLAÇA DE LLUIS MILLET

CARRER DE SANT PERE MÉS ALT

AV. DE FRANCESC CAMBO

VIA LAIETANA

PLAÇA DE CATALUNYA

Pause in **PLAÇA DE CATALUNYA** 5

mire the monument to Catalan republican president Francesc Macià i Llussa. It mbolizes the causes he ght for: republicanism and socialism.

4

Give a nod to the **HOTEL CONTINENTAL**

Pass the hotel where George Orwell wrote *Homage to Catalonia*; it was here that he nursed wounds he'd amassed while fighting for the Republic.

Walk through **PLAÇA DE SANT FELIP NERI**

The buildings surrounding this square are pockmarked with shrapnel holes, remnants of an Italian bombardment, in 1938, that killed 42 people.

LA RAMBLA

CARRER D'ELISABETS

CARRER DE LA PORTAFERRISSA

CARRER DEL PI

CARRER DE ST HONORAT

2

3

CARRER DE JAUME I

CARRER DEL CARME

Enjoy a sweet treat at **CAELUM**

Take a break at Caelum (Latin for "heaven"). Everything here is baked by Spanish monks and nuns.

GOTHIC QUARTER

1

Start your journey at **PALAU DE LA GENERALITAT DE CATALUNYA**

Take in the offices of the Catalan Government, the institution of which was abolished under Franco in 1940. An underground air raid shelter was unearthed here a few years ago.

CARRER DE FERRAN

RAVAL

CARRER DE L'HOSPITAL

Finish up at **BAR MARSELLA**

You've earned a drink. Reflect on your day at Bar Marsella, where Civil War correspondent Ernest Hemingway spent many an evening.

LA RAMBLA

PLAÇA REIAL

RAMBLA DEL RAVAL

7

| 0 metres | | 200 |
| 0 yards | | 200 |

NIGHTLIFE

Life doesn't stop when the sun goes down in Barna – if anything, it just gets started. Nights pass hopping between sultry terraces, legendary queer bars and revelrous clubs.

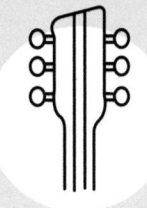  

LGBTQ+ Scene

On paper, Spain is one of the most Catholic countries in Europe – and it's also one of the most LGBTQ+-friendly. However you identify, Barcelona will welcome you with open arms.

LA CHAPELLE

Map 4; Carrer de Muntaner, 67, Eixample; ///closed.bluntly.acting; 934 533 076

Nowhere embodies Spain's contradiction of Catholic and queer better than La Chapelle. Decked out with more Catholic iconography than you can shake a crosier at, the Eixample club could have been the setting of Madonna's *Like a Prayer* video. Be sure to arrive early to get in (by early, we mean 10pm).

SAFARI DISCO CLUB

Map 3; Carrer de Tarragona, 141, Sants; ///burns.migrants.leave; www.safaridiscoclub.com

A lot of clubs were victims of the pandemic but LGBTQ+ stronghold Safari Disco Club is still standing. Come the weekend, this is where Barna's queer community head for reliable club nights, dancing their troubles away to reggaeton, house and, of course, classic club hits.

CANDY DARLING

Map 4; Gran Via de les Corts Catalanes, 586, Sant Antoni;
///honestly.safe.mouse

You know a bar is well versed in its queer history when pink triangles
– once a Nazi badge of shame – are reclaimed to signal LGBTQ+
pride. Named after American trans icon Candy Darling, this unusually
roomy (for Barna) bar is the place of choice for out-and-proud locals.
Expect a line-up of experimental queer artists and plenty of voguing.

CARITA BONITA

Map 4; Carrer de Balmes, 69, Eixample; ///thunder.teaches.tonight;
685 999 635

Split into different areas, Barcelona's lesbian bar *par excellence* is
whatever you need it to be. Looking to catch up with a friend over a
mojito? There's a laid-back space for that. You and the gang planning
to dance the night away? Carita Bonita's dance floor won't disappoint.
» Don't leave without chatting to the bar staff – Carita Bonita has
some of the friendliest in the city.

EL CANGREJO

Map 2; Carrer de Montserrat 9, Raval; ///active.grades.acrobat; 933 012 978

Nights out don't get more in-your-face than at this bastion of queer
culture. Like their sisters who performed here in the 1990s, drag acts
draw heavily on local pop culture and flamenco, and are obsessed
with Spanish divas. They love a lewd joke, too, and will pull audience
members up on stage. You've been warned.

MADAME JASMINE

Map 2; Rambla del Raval, 22, Raval; ///boarding.custard.gives

Tiger-print fur on the wall, fringed lamps hanging from the ceiling and bartenders wrapped in capes and shawls: Madame Jasmine is the underground of the queer scene. This deliciously debauched bar is the go-to for Barcelona's rag-tag crowd of gutterpunks, who take advantage of the communal pots of glitter and rhinestones to get themselves looking the part, all while sipping potent cocktails.

» Don't leave without visiting the toilet to read printouts of the bar's (few) bad online reviews lining the bathroom walls.

LA FEDERICA

Map 3; Carrer de Salvà 3, Poble Sec; ///humans.gearing.relax

Looking for something a bit more chilled? Seventies-themed La Federica is the best spot to nurse a beer in the company of a laid-back crowd. Chat to the bar staff about the bar's latest art exhibition (most artworks on the walls are for sale) or swing by for a charity drag bingo night (just make sure you can count from *uno* to *cien*).

BELIEVE CLUB

Map 4; Carrer de Balmes 56, Eixample; ///glitter.palaces.darkest; www.thebelieve.club

Things get going around midnight at Barcelona's drag cabaret and continue into the early hours. Sure, this LGBTQ+ club doesn't break the mould with its choice of music, but on those nights when you just need a beer and a dance, Believe delivers.

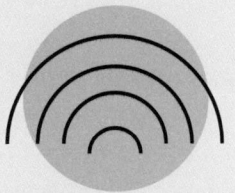

Liked by the locals

"Barcelona's drag and queer scene has a huge range of options – from Believe, where you'll see the next generation of drag acts, to Ocaña, where the city's living legends perform. But if you want to discover real Barcelona, head to Madame Jasmine for the underground queer scene."

TONI SOBRINO/VILMA PORUX, DRAG ARTIST

Cool Clubs

Ask any southern European and they'll tell you that Barna is the place to go clubbing. Be sure to have an afternoon siesta before a big night out, mind; the party really gets going around 2am, after all.

APOLO

Map 3; Carrer Nou de la Rambla, 113, Poble Sec; ///pipeline.respond.bundles; www.sala-apolo.com

If Barcelona is a clubbing capital, then Apolo is its royal palace. Once upon a time this grand ballroom was the crowning glory of the theatre scene around Avinguda del Paral·lel. Now discerning Barcelonans dance under its chandeliers to the beats of the most prestigious names in dance music at weekend club nights.

RAZZMATAZZ

Map 5; Carrer dels Almogàvers, 122, Poblenou; ///exact.cookery.pancake; www.salarazzmatazz.com

We know, we know, a club in an old factory is nothing new but the scale of Razzmatazz is truly something to behold. With all the grimy-chic trimmings you'd expect of a post-industrial setting, this heavy-weight has five party rooms (six if you count the toilet where

DJ sets sometimes take place), each with its own personality. Depending on the night, the rooms throughout this giant space reverberate with the sounds of anything from hardcore techno to synth-powered 80s classics.

» Don't leave without hanging around on the terraces that link the rooms at Razzmatazz; it's the best place to make friends, especially if you have a cigarette to give away.

MOOG

Map 2; Carrer de l'Arc del Teatre, 3, Raval; ///hope.bouncing.casually; www.moogbarcelona.com

It might be the size of a postage stamp but there's always enough space at Moog. Two-step on inside and you'll first be met by hardcore ravers headbanging to techno blaring from one of the best sound systems in the city. Continue upstairs where a hall of mirrors forms the stage for resident DJ Purpur, who plays favourite 80s and 90s hits while doing Beyoncé-style hairography in front of a fan.

SALA UPLOAD

Map 3; Avinguda de Francesc Ferrer i Guàrdia, 13, Montjuïc; ///alien.hillside.wounds; www.sala-upload.com

Housed within the historic Poble Espanyol, Sala Upload is the ultimate underground club spot. It's all about giving a platform to marginalized communities, whether that's on the decks or on the dancefloor. Party people get down at regular events, from women-led club nights to sets hosted by queer collectives – there really is something for everyone here.

LA TERRRAZZA

Map 3; Avinguda Francesc Ferrer i Guàrdia s/n, Montjuïc;
///hedge.leaflet.waddle; www.laterrrazza.com

What could be more magical than dancing the night away under the stars? We know: dancing under the stars at a replica 16th-century farmhouse surrounded by palm trees. Yes, La Terrrazza might be awash with international crowds rather than born-and-bred Barcelonans, making the drink prices a little higher than at other clubs. But the setting!

LA PALOMA

Map 2; Carrer del Tigre, 27, Raval; ///flute.endings.cloak; www.lapaloma.com

After a 15-year hiatus due to noise complaints, this mainstay of Barna nightlife is back. The décor – all chandeliers and frescoes – might feel old, but the music here is as fresh as it gets. These days, La Paloma runs an earlier schedule, with things winding down at 3am – perfect for a warm-up sesh (or for those who can't hack staying out any later).

» Don't leave without keeping it quiet on the way out – we don't want another decade without our favourite ballroom.

MARULA CAFÉ

Map 1; Carrer dels Escudellers, 49, Gothic Quarter;
///earliest.smoking.refuse; www.marulacafe.com

Velvet bar-stools, rich red curtains and a disco ball hanging from the ceiling: retro Marula Café is one classy joint. The music is just as elegant, with an owner of Barcelona City Records *(p100)* frequently

Marula Café is very popular with Barcelonans so get here around 1am to secure your patch.

starring as DJ. He spins disco, funk, afrobeat and soul records on vinyl – *always* on vinyl – to an appreciative crowd of music connoisseurs.

LAUT

Map 3; Carrer de Vila i Vilà, 63, Poble Sec; ///organs.communal.pilots; www.laut.es

The best things in life come in small packages. Take Laut, a little avant-garde club that punches above its weight thanks to its killer sound system (hinted at in its name; *laut* means "loud" in German). After a hard week at work, the city's coolest lace up their favourite trainers and make for a night out here, safe in the knowledge that Laut will deliver a carefully curated experimental programme of up-and-coming names on the electronic scene.

MACARENA CLUB

Map 1; Carrer Nou de Sant Francesc, 5, Gothic Quarter; ///goals.slippery.design; www.macarenaclub.com

First things first, you're not going to be dancing the Macarena here, despite the club's name. That is unless you can make your aunt's favourite dance moves match some of the hardest hitting house and techno baselines in the city (doubtful). Macarena Club is unusually convivial for a hardcore techno club (not to mention very small) so you'll likely find yourself making new friends as you live your best life on the dance floor.

Late-Night Bars

Big night out ahead? Fancy one more drink before bed? Barna has loads of late-night bars where locals keep the party going, which – given that clubbing doesn't really get going until late – is a godsend.

NEVERMIND

Map 2; Carrer dels Tallers, 68, Raval; ///herds.release.status; 663 710 095

Ever feel the urge to ditch your drink for your board? Barcelonans sure do – skating is a big deal here in Barna – and Nevermind is on hand for those moments. This gritty spot in Raval is a skater's

Hidden away down a tiny alleyway in uber-trendy Gràcia lies Musical Maria *(Carrer de Maria, 5)*. Can't spot it? Look for the omnipresent crowd of smokers hanging around the door. The dive bar is a literal temple to rock music (don't expect any club hits here), its walls covered in shrine-like music memorabilia. Make yourself at home with the motley crew of punters, all swigging beer and swapping life stories across the stained pool table.

paradise, with its indoor half-pipe, graffiti-splattered walls and soundtrack of crunchy grunge. Not a skateboarder? Fear not. Skaters are only too happy to provide some late-night entertainment while you kick-back with a (dirt-cheap) beer.

OCAÑA

Map 1; Plaça Reial, 13–15, Gothic Quarter; ///invite.printers.hiking;
www.ocana.cat

When the locals are feeling fancy and want to flaunt it, LGBTQ+ bar Ocaña is where they go. Those looking for a sedate drink settle in on the decadent ground floor, which is all stylish candelabras and exposed beams. Beneath their feet, things are much more lively in the basement (aren't they always?) thanks to DJ sets and live performances. With cocktails flowing and plenty of space to dance, even those upstairs are tempted below deck to let out their wilder side.

FOXY BAR

Map 2; Carrer de la Riera Alta, 59, Raval; ///popping.dishes.paves;
www.foxybarbcn.wixsite.com

Foxy might look like your grandma's living room, with its vintage flock wallpaper and chintzy furniture, but Raval locals know it as a vibey bar – just the job for a date. Order a couple of mojitos, recline on plush chaise longes and while away what remains of the night trying to decipher the quirky paraphernalia hanging from the walls.
» Don't leave without stopping in at Els Tres Tombs, around the corner. It's a great place to people-watch Barcelona's night owls.

GUZZO CLUB

Map 1; Plaça Comercial, 10, Born; ///clocks.harvest.pound;
www.guzzorestaurante.es

Early evening is dinnertime at Guzzo Club but as midnight ticks
closer the place transforms into a late-night party. Diners get tipsy
on creative cocktails, and cool kids turn up for the live jazz acts. The
whole place has a wonderfully artsy feel, with upcycled furniture
and graffiti-covered walls (often painted to a live audience).

» Don't leave without having a bite here; the dishes are truly
gourmet and beautifully presented.

CURTIS AUDIOPHILE CAFÉ

Map 4; Carrer de Mallorca, 196, Eixample; ///unusually.fended.gross;
www.curtisaudiocafe.com

It's all about the sanctity of music at this late-night café. Top-notch
speakers surround the bar, DJs perform curated sets and boxes of
records wait to be rummaged through. Order a vermouth and
make use of the vinyl listening stations.

POLAROID BAR

Map 1; Carrer dels Còdols, 29, Gothic Quarter; ///tenses.juniors.prop;
www.polaroidbar.es

Hop into your DeLorean or, failing that, hail a taxi: we're going back
to the 80s. Sure, the Space Invaders murals, ET bike hanging from
the ceiling and VHS tapes plastered across the walls are bordering
on tacky, but what's wrong with that? If you need help getting into

Want more retro shenanigans? Turn up on a Sunday night for hotdogs and cult movie screenings.

the mood, take a look at Polaroid's menu of kitsch cocktails – perhaps try a *Flashdance* with cachaça and passionfruit or a fittingly red, vodka-based *Beetlejuice*.

MANCHESTER

Map 1; Carrer de Milans, 5, Gothic Quarter; ///gushes.camps.judge; www.manchesterbar.com

Yes, this one is a bit of a dive: the walls are plastered with ageing band memorabilia, sticky tables pepper the place and the smell of spilled beer lingers in the air. But that's all part of the charm. Paying homage to Britain's music-making city of Manchester, this buzzy bar is the last stop of the night for Barcelona's die-hard indie fans and Anglophiles alike. Together they bop down memory lane to the soundtrack of Joy Division, The Smiths and The Stone Roses.

33/45

Map 2; Carrer de Joaquín Costa, 4, Raval; ///averts.passes.gloves; www.3345.es

After-hours drinks don't have to be raucous. Take this low-key spot, where scenesters break up the night before hitting the next bar. They sink gratefully into the bar's leather armchairs and sofas (no booze-soaked barrels to crane over or wonky stools to teeter on here), sip 33/45's famous tequila cocktails and gaze dreamily at the for-sale artworks dotted across the walls.

Live Music

People from all walks of life gather in Barcelona's live music venues, all looking to be carried away by the music. And with everything from jazz to flamenco, there's a show for every night of the week.

VOL

Map 5; Carrer de Sancho de Ávila 78, Poble Nou; ///soldiers.aimless. dangerously; www.salavol.com

If niche music genres are your thing, make your way to Vol. A hub of grunge nestled among the glassy façades of Barcelona's emerging corporate district, this cooperative-run venue hosts under-the-radar musicians playing genres you've probably never heard. Expect a roster of acts performing everything from Belorussian post-punk to Peruvian hardcore.

L'AUDITORI

Map 5; Carrer de Lepant 150, Glòries; ///terminal.erupts.record; www.auditori.cat

While Palau de la Música Catalana *(p121)* hogs the limelight, L'Auditori humbly goes about its business, offering the best acoustics in the city, whatever the genre. Yes, the modern music hall isn't as pretty as its

Modernista cousin, but the overshadowed spot is all about delivering what the people deserve: world-class music. Classical music is the main player, but pop, rock, folk and electronica concerts also appear on L'Auditori's first-class music programme.

» **Don't leave without** making a stop at the Museu de la Música inside L'Auditori to learn about all things music history.

HELIOGÀBAL

Map 4; Carrer de Ramón y Cajal, 80, Gràcia; ///spits.pursuit.solo; www.heliogabal.com

At this music bar, up-and-coming acts are known to lay down tunes before they make it big. Pop in for a beer with Barcelona's die-hard music lovers on the lookout for their new favourite band. Who knows? In a few years' time you might spot some familiar faces on the main stage of Primavera Sound.

Shh!

Let's keep this between us, *sí*? For some truly local music, make 23 Robadors a port of call *(www.23robadors. com)*. Squeeze your way into this little rock-walled cave with its low-hanging beams (tall friends, beware) for a rowdy night of jazz, live Latin sounds and flamenco; we say flamenco but we don't mean the touristy polka-dot-dress-and-castanets kind, rather the very real, very emotional kind. Pair with well-priced beers and nibbles and you've got a night to remember.

Solo, Pair, Crowd

Whether you've got a few hours to yourself or you're craving a night out with the gang, Barcelona's music scene has got you covered.

FLYING SOLO

Art and a show

When a date with yourself is long overdue, make for Museu Europeu d'Art Modern in Born. Explore the museum on a Friday or Saturday before checking out the museum's little-known music programme.

IN A PAIR

Spine-tingling strings

Treat a special someone to an evening of candlelit classical guitar music in the Santa Maria del Pi church in the Gothic Quarter. Goosebumps are guaranteed.

FOR A CROWD

Groove with the gang

With live music and plenty of space to dance, Quilombo in Eixample is the ideal place for a night with your besties. As it's a dive bar, the drinks are wallet-friendly so you can party guilt-free into the early hours.

JAMBOREE JAZZ

Map 1; Plaça Reial, 17, Gothic Quarter; ///inhaled.crab.loosed;
www.jamboreejazz.com

A basement setting, crumbling brick walls, moody lighting: Jamboree would have all the trappings of a clandestine bar were it not one of the best-loved live music joints in the city. This local legend has kept Barna swinging since the 60s, when the likes of Bill Coleman, Kenny Drew and Dexter Gordon graced the pocket-sized stage. A Monday night Jamboree jam session is a rite of passage in Barcelona, attracting seasoned listeners and fresh-faced newbies alike.

» **Don't leave without** heading over to tapas bar Palosanto post-jam to wind up your evening with some drinks and sharing plates.

EL GRAN TEATRE DEL LICEU

Map 2; La Rambla, 51–59, Raval; ///molars.defining.libraries;
www.liceubarcelona.cat

For all their love of techno and electronic music, Barcelonans are partial to a bit of Puccini, especially in their city's opera house, of which they're hugely proud. And we can see why: the palatial theatre has survived fires, bombings, the Civil War, COVID-19. Speaking of, it was during the pandemic that the Liceu made headlines by staging a concert for 2,300 house plants (all of which were given to healthcare workers). Today, Barcelonans are grateful to be back in the plush red chairs, watching classics like *Carmen*, *La Bohème* and *Die Walküre*. The under-35s among you: keep an eye out for under-35 events, when a night at the opera (for a special price) is followed by drinks and a DJ set up on the opera house roof.

Night Terraces

Sultry summers melt into temperate winters in Barcelona. Whatever the season, locals gravitate towards outdoor terraces to spend unhurried evenings with loved ones under the stars.

BAR CENTRAL

Map 2; Carrer d'Elisabets, 6, Raval; ///smooth.enhancement.applies; www.barcentral.bar

Looking for a laid-back spot? Make a beeline for this lush, plant-filled patio bar set in the back of a bookshop. University grads and intellectuals are regulars at this terrace, once the courtyard of an abbot's palace. Draw up a chair alongside them and drink in their spirited conversations over a glass of rioja.

ANTIC TEATRE

Map 1; Carrer de Verdaguer i Callís, 12, Born; ///smoke.bucked.bubbles; www.anticteatre.com

This vibey terrace, set in the courtyard of a theatre, has become a total hit with the locals. Sure, the furniture has seen better days, but the fairy lights strung up in the trees, the cheap beers and candles on the tables more than make up for it. A word to the wise:

If the terrace is full, walk round the corner to Plaça de Sant Pere, a charming medieval square.

if you head inside to order at the bar while there's a performance on, you will be hastily told to shh (it's happened to the best of us).

CÀMPING

Map 5; Carrer de Carmen Amaya, 18, Poblenou;
///decks.fizzy.watched

On a balmy night, this is the place to be. Gaggles of rowdy pals congregate at this campsite-inspired (and ultra-hipster) terrace with street food pop-ups and a strict zero-waste policy. Stretched out on the communal picnic blankets, the footloose and fancy-free clink beers and compete with other drinkers to set the music on the terrace's online jukebox. Camping has never been so fun.

» Don't leave without challenging your mates – or a friendly local – to a round of ping-pong. Ask for balls and bats at the bar.

BAR CALDERS

Map 3; Carrer del Parlament, 25, Sant Antoni; ///harvest.timidly.trifle;
933 299 349

Named after a beloved Catalan author, Bar Calders is tucked away on a little side street, giving its terrace a deliciously undiscovered feel (no *guiris* in sight). Sant Antoni locals hoof it here for an evening vermouth or a signature gin and tonic, which comes in a satisfying goldfish-bowl-sized glass. Be sure to visit earlier in the evening because once regulars get a table, they're not giving it up easily.

MESCLADÍS DEL POU

Map 1; Carrer dels Carders, 35, Born; ///searches.trouble.admire;
www. mescladis.org

Set in a patio connecting two of Born's streets of medieval arches
and balconies, this terrace is about as picturesque as it gets. Not that
it's all about good looks here. The buzzy bar is local to the core, run
by a group that helps undocumented migrants find their feet in the
service sector.

TERRASSA DE LES INDIANES

Map 5; Plaça Pau Vila, 3, Barceloneta; ///other.egging.shoving;
www.1881persagardi.com

Catalonia's National History Museum conceals a secret – and it's
not one you might expect. Make your way to the top floor, where
you'll find a hidden restaurant and, within it, the swish Terrassa de
les Indianes. Sip on a decadent drink with views every which way
you look: Montjuïc slipping down into the sea, the waving sails of Port
Vell, night falling over the rooftops of the Gothic Quarter, it's all there.

Try it!
DANCE WITH THE STARS

Barna is big on swing – you'll likely see
locals dancing in the street. Join the friendly
folk at Swing Maniacs (*www.swingmaniacs.
com*) for a masterclass and dance the night
away at La Caseta del Migdia.

OK, we'll admit it's a bougier affair than other terraces, but those views make it worth it.

LA MONROE

Map 5; Plaça de Salvador Seguí 1, Raval; ///zipped.maple.nagging; www.lamonroe.es

The bar of the Filmoteca de Catalunya (p131), La Monroe is a favourite alfresco drink spot in the heart of Raval. Its swish, industrial-chic interior makes way for a roomy terrace, where groups of pals get together for a drink most days of the week. On weekends, DJs start to spin records and the crowd gets bigger as the night draws in. It's as effortlessly cool as the film aficionado crowd it attracts.

SALTS

Map 3; Avinguda Miramar, 31, Montjuïc; ///ripples.poker.perky; www.saltsmontjuic.com

As the sun sets over Barcelona, the city's seagull population comes to roost on the Olympic diving pools (p175). Meanwhile, above the bleachers, things are in full swing on the terrace at Salts. Like the clamouring sports fans of 30 years ago, young people pour in expectantly, chatting excitedly to their friends. They're here for one thing and one thing only: to watch the last rays of sun colour the roofs of the city as dusk falls, drink in hand. Life is good.

» **Don't leave without** jumping on the Montjuïc funicular railway to take you back down to the city (it's included in the price of a metro ticket).

Built in the 1990s to revitalize Raval, today **MACBA** is known for its skaters outside. People come from all over to show what they can do.

PLAÇA DELS ÀNGELS

CARRER DEL CARME

LA RAMBL.

Chow down at
BISMILLAH KEBABISH

Most nights out end at Bismillah, the best of Raval's kebab shops. Sit in or get a tasty chicken wrap for the trip home.

PLAÇA DE LA GARDUNYA

3

4

CARRER DE JOAQUÍN COSTA

Refuel at
BAR FIDEL

Step inside the cave-like Bar Fidel and refuel with one of the bar's classic baguette sandwiches.

CARRER DE LA RIERA ALTA

CARRER DE MARIA AURÈLIA CAPMANY

CARRER DE L'HOSPITAL

Like many of its neighbours, the giant iron cat **El Gat de Botero** searched for a home for ages before finding its place in Raval.

PLAÇA DEL PEDRÓ

RAVAL

CARRER DE LA RIERETA

RAMBLA DEL RAVAL

CARRER

2

Live it up at
MADAME JASMINE

Head to Madame Jasmine, where the music's loud and the outfits are louder. This bar shirks gender norms, so don't be afraid of wearing something a little risqué.

Kick off the night at
LA CASA DE LA PRADERA

Start with a beer at this welcoming queer bar. Order filling Mediterranean fare from the menu at Las Fernandez, just next door, and tuck in on La Casa's terrace (the bars are good pals).

CARRER DE SANTA ELENA

1

0 metres	100
0 yards	100

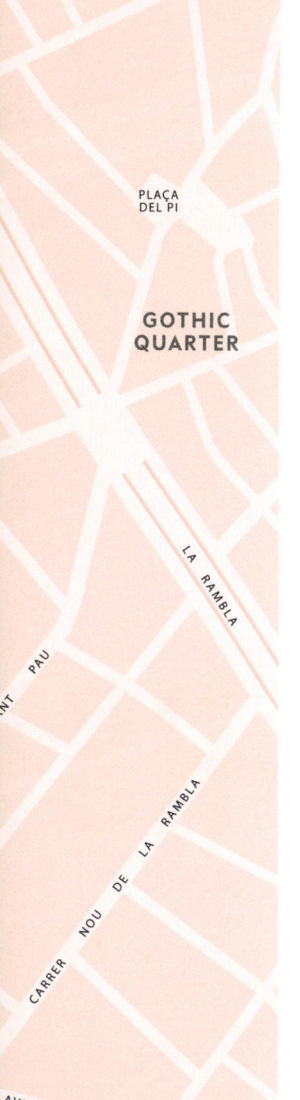

PLAÇA DEL PI

GOTHIC QUARTER

LA RAMBLA

ANT PAU

CARRER NOU DE LA RAMBLA

AVINGUDA DE LES DRASSANES

A night out in
revelrous Raval

No matter who you are, there's a space for you in Raval. Like much here, the *barri's* name comes from somewhere else – specifically the word *rabad*, which translates as "neighbourhood" in Arabic. And the area is defined by the various communities who have come to call it home: immigrants and anarchists, outcasts and outlaws, artists and activists. Once a no-go for tourists, Raval has transformed into a thriving area that represents the heart of Barcelona's rebellious spirit. Streets are safer and cultural institutions have opened but the *barri* remains revolutionary.

1. La Casa de la Pradera
Carrer de les Carretes, 57;
625 232 755
///typist.goods.shiver

2. Madame Jasmine
Rambla del Raval, 22;
///boarding.custard.gives

3. Bar Fidel
Carrer de Ferlandina, 24;
933 041 439
////bedrock.fever.move

4. Bismillah Kebabish
Carrer de Joaquín Costa, 22;
934 430 184
///barman.swanky.pies

El Gat de Botero
///spits.dampen.shaky

MACBA
///cutaway.unrealistic.frost

OUTDOORS

Waves lapping the shore, lush green spaces, buzzing public squares: it's not just year-round sun that tempts locals to while away their days outdoors.

Beautiful Beaches

Whatever the season, locals gravitate towards the beach. Sure, some are overrun with tourists (and, yes, their litter) but there are hidden spots that Barcelonans love, and you'll fall for, too.

PLATJA DE MONTGAT

Entrance via Carrer del Mar, Montgat; ///that.milkman.rosette; www.montgat.cat

At long last, the weekend has arrived! Pack a bag and get a good night's sleep; in the morning, you're catching a train to the city's outer fringes for a day at Montgat beach. Perhaps you'll rent a dinghy and bob about on the crystal clear water, or make a start on that novel under the shade of a beach umbrella. Either way, life doesn't get much better.

» Don't leave without keeping yourself going with some snacks and drinks at beach bar Banys Verge del Carme *(p51)*.

PLATJA DEL GARRAF

Entrance via Garraf Station, El Garraf;
///establishing.avocados.barging

A gorgeous secluded cove bounded by green-and-white-striped beach huts awaits after a short train ride from Barna. With some of the cleanest waters, and overlooked by the mountains of the Garraf Massif, Platja del Garraf feels a world away from the hubbub of the city. It's a quiet retreat, where dog walkers track up and down the beach, their dogs skipping in and out of the water, and couples walk hand-in-hand on sunset strolls.

BANYS DEL FÒRUM

Entrance via Parc del Fòrum, Fòrum; ///globe.brief.prestige

Okay, this one technically isn't a beach but for those who hate the feeling of sand in their clothes, Barcelona's saltwater lido is a happy alternative. Time your arrival for sunset, when this urban expanse of concrete blocks and solar panels makes for a strangely beautiful, dusky scene. The summer-only lido is cast in the Mediterranean Sea so you might even see a couple of octopuses or turtles swim past as you enjoy an evening dip.

PLATJA DE LES FILIPINES

Access via Avinguda de Europa, Viladecans; ///milkman.jokers.haggle;
www.viladecans.cat

The bus journey here may be on the longer side (it's a 45-minute ride away from the centre), but it's worth it when you reach the sweeping expanse of yellow sand and lapping waves of Platja de les Filipines. Rolling dunes and the Remolar nature reserve around the Llobregat Delta provide a welcome dose of nature, while the hum of incoming planes is a reminder that the city is not far at all.

PLATJA DE SANT SEBASTIÀ AND PLATJA DE SANT MIQUEL

Entrance via Passeig Marítim, Barceloneta;
///verge.mailer.rugs

We've all thought it: city life can be stressful. Sometimes you just need to let your hair down and hang loose. On such days, clothing-optional Sant Sebastià, a stone's throw from the city, is just the ticket. Having trouble finding a spot? Prefer not to bare all?

Try it!
BEACH CLEAN

Tourism ravages Barna's beaches, especially those of Barceloneta. Do your part on a Saturday morning and join a beach clean. You'll likely make some friends along the way (www.cleanbeachinitiative.org).

No fear: you get two beaches in one here in Barceloneta. Stroll along the sand to sister beach Sant Miquel for a restorative blast of sea air with slightly different views.

>> Don't leave without pausing for thought at the Som i Serem Ciutat Refugi memorial, which honours the refugees who have died in their attempt to cross the Mediterranean to find a new home.

PLATJA DE LA MAR BELLA

Entrance via Passeig Marítim del Bogatell, Poblenou;
///singles.respond.imitate

Created around the time of the Olympics, Mar Bella is Barna's de facto LGBTQ+ beach, replete with its own "BeGay" beach bar. Prepare for a lot of nakedness – Mar Bella is also one of the city's nudist beaches (when it comes to beach days, Catalans love to get their kit off). Your birthday suit isn't compulsory, mind, so you're more than welcome to keep your swimwear on. You do you.

PLATJA D'OCATA

Entrance via Passeig Marítim, Masnou; ///transmitted.wink.replace;
www.masnou.cat

A bright, sunny day and crisp paperback are all it takes to persuade urbanites to journey to Ocata, just outside the city. They sprawl out on the sand and languidly watch the waters lap along the picture-postcard beach, no *guiris* in sight. Sounds good, doesn't it? And it's definitely worth the extra 20 minutes on the train to reach it.

City Squares

Barcelona's squares are cornerstones of their **barris.** *It's in these public spaces that neighbours chitchat, friends rendezvous and grandparents watch the world go by.*

PLAÇA DE LA ROSA DELS VENTS
Map 5; access via Passeig de Joan de Borbó, Barceloneta;
///identity.hiding.madness

Ask a local what they think of the W Hotel and they'll either tell you it's an iconic point on the city skyline or a total eyesore. The one thing that everyone agrees on, though, is that the square behind the hotel is utterly idyllic. Looking out onto the Mediterranean, it's the perfect place to park up with pals and watch the sun slip behind the horizon.

SUPERILLA PARLAMENT/BORRELL
Map 3; Carrer del Parlament, 39, Sant Antoni;
///liners.secret.tweeted

Barcelona's progressive mayor Ada Colau made it her mission to make Barna more sustainable. Under her guidance, the city council set about tackling carbon emissions by closing roads around the city's grid system and opening up pavement space for the community.

Experience the *superilla* (superblock) scheme for yourself at the crossing of Carrer Comte Borrell and Carrer del Parlament. Here, old boys battle it out at the public chess tables, parents sip *orxatas* as their children let off steam and home workers enjoy a much needed break away from their screens.

» **Don't leave without** stopping by Horchatería Sirvent for tasty ice creams and *orxatas*.

PLAÇA DELS ÀNGELS

Map 2; Plaça dels Àngels, Raval; ///caveman.themes.daily

Barcelonans of all ages can be spotted commuting around the city by skateboard, or stopping for coffee with a board tucked under their arm. There are various skateparks dotted around the city but the hub of skate culture is Plaça dels Àngels, more commonly known as "Plaça del MACBA". Skaters take advantage of MACBA's expanse of concrete, drops and steps, all to an audience of appreciative onlookers.

JARDINS DE RUBIÓ I LLUCH

Map 2; Carrer de l'Hospital, 56, Raval; ///players.fixated.bombard

When the intensity of Raval is a bit much, seek sanctuary in the tranquil Jardins de Rubió i Lluch. Set around a trickling fountain, this pretty walled square is favoured by students from the nearby Massana art school and those stopping for a breather en route to MACBA. In summer, the square runs a free book exchange, so you can select a scintillating novel to read under the square's fragrant orange trees.

PLAÇA DE LA VILA DE GRÀCIA

Map 4; Plaça de la Vila de Gràcia, Gràcia; ///stadium.bakers.salsa

If there's one thing that Barcelonans love to do of an afternoon, it's chill out at a pavement café with friends and a couple of *canyes*. When it comes to choosing a square for such an occasion, Gràcia locals are spoiled for choice but Plaça de la Vila takes some beating. With its pretty chiming clock tower and numerous cafés, this lovely spot is the perfect setting to quaff a glass of beer and let the conversation flow freely.

PLAÇA DEL SOL

Map 4; Plaça del Sol, Gràcia; ///hoot.slipped.behaving

Gràcia has a reputation as Barcelona's hippie hub and nowhere embodies this better than Plaça del Sol. A bohemian crowd sit on the ground in the centre of the square, strumming guitars and sketching the scene around them. Join them at it – or swap the hard concrete for the comfort of a nearby pavement café.

» Don't leave without picking up a book at the square's charming second-hand bookshop, Saturnàlia.

PLAÇA DE SANT FELIP NERI

Map 1; Plaça de Sant Felip Neri, Gothic Quarter; ///squeezed.scout.swept

On weekdays, at 5pm, tiny Plaça de Sant Felip Neri suddenly fills with the excited clamour of school kids swarming out of the school on the square, all chuffed to be heading home or to an *orxateria*.

The rest of the day, this medieval courtyard – sandwiched between the cathedral and the Palau de la Generalitat – remains quiet. It's eerie and haunting, like it's clinging to the past tragedies witnessed here. After all, the buildings of this little square are pockmarked from Civil War bombings. There's no drinking in this square; this is the place for some meditative time alone.

PLAÇA DE SANT AGUSTÍ VELL

Map 1; Plaça de Sant Agustí Vell, Born;
///hilltop.letters.discrepancy

Part-square, part-promenade, Sant Agustí Vell stretches from the Santa Maria del Mar church to Born's former central market. During the day it's the passing place of Barcelona's hoi polloi, all busy running errands and going hurriedly about their business. When night falls, the place transforms. Punters pause at the square's bars, spilling out onto the cobblestones where they nurse glasses of wine under the streetlamps.

PLAÇA DEL PI

Map 1; Plaça del Pi, Gothic Quarter; ///averages.adjusted.nuggets

City squares don't get more charming than this spot in the Gothic Quarter. At its heart is the Basilica de Santa Maria del Pi, which watches protectively over the locals scoffing tapas in the square below. Twice a month, patrons leave their seats for the Catalan food market that sets up shop here, filling their bags with cheese, wine and chocolate and chatting to the stall owners like old friends.

Outdoor Activities

The 1992 Olympics inspired a long-lasting relationship with keeping fit. And what better place to exercise than outdoors? The temperate climate here makes this a year-round reality.

ESPIGÓ DEL GAS

Map 5; entrance via Passeig Marítim de la Barceloneta, Barceloneta; ///fracture.receive.suckle

Barna is big on giving locals space to work out for free. Take this breakwater with its own outdoor gym, where fitness fanatics work on their strength and toning, all the while keeping cool in the sea breeze. Get here early in the morning to avoid the crowds and, more importantly, the blistering summer heat.

INERCIA ROLLERBLADE RENTAL

Map 5; Carrer de Roger de Flor, 10, Ciutadella; ///managers.arching.fade; www.inercia.com

Make like it's the 90s and don your Rollerblades, or rent a pair from Inercia for a few euros. Weave your way round the Ciutadella park *(p176)*, through the oh-so-cool Barceloneta neighbourhood and all the way down to the locals' favourite blading spot: the

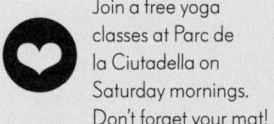 Join a free yoga classes at Parc de la Ciutadella on Saturday mornings. Don't forget your mat!

seafront promenade. Here you'll find the paved, palm-tree-lined shoreline (perfect for beachside blading) and lots of places to stop for a refreshing fruit juice.

PARC DE L'ESPANYA INDUSTRIAL

Map 6; entrance via Carrer de Muntades, Sants; ///overtime.marked.lion

Ever heard of *pilota*? Locals can't get enough of this Basque/Valencian handball sport. It's a little bit like squash, but instead of using a racket to hit a ball against a wall (called a *frontón*) you use your hands. The best spot for a game of *pilota*? Otherworldly Parc de l'Espanya Industrial could have been plucked from a sci-fi film, and offers a one-of-a-kind *frontón* setting. Those looking for a more familiar sport, rest assured: there's also basketball courts and table-tennis tables here.

» Don't leave without cooling off on the bleachers and admiring the amazing views of the artificial lake.

BARCELONA BEACH HOUSE

Map 5; Avinguda Litoral, 78, Poblenou; ///bricks.airbag.fits; www.barcelonabeachhouse.com

What could be more relaxing than saluting the sun to the sound of breaking waves? Barcelona Beach House is just the place for some much needed zen, holding English-language yoga classes near Mar Bella beach (*p167*). Haven't packed your mat? No problem: you can rent one for the session.

Solo, Pair, Crowd

Chasing a new PB? Looking to workout with your bestie? Prefer to pair sport with a little refreshment? Barcelona's got an activity just for you.

FLYING SOLO

A run with a view

Head up to the mountains for a jog along the Carretera de las Aigües. This lovely running route stretches out along the city and winds its way through small wooded areas, promising incredible views.

IN A PAIR

Soulful surfing

Grab your bestie and head down to Surf House Barcelona to find your feet on a paddleboard. Debrief on your adventure with a healthy(ish) brunch in the California-style surf shack after.

FOR A CROWD

Table tennis tournament

You'll spot ping pong tables across the city – locals are obsessed. Challenge your friends to a championship over a few drinks at Càmping *(p157)*.

PISCINA MUNICIPAL MONTJUÏC

Map 3; Avinguda Miramar 31, Montjuïc; ///lamps.rejoin.career

Those wanting to relive the glory years make like Olympians at the summertime diving pools up on Montjuïc. They swim lengths with the city as a stunning backdrop, then it's time to dry off in the sun with a few poolside card games. Who said workouts were hard?

» Don't leave without having a well-earned snack at the Salts *(p159)* above the swimming pools.

SKATEPARK MAR BELLA

Map 5; entrance via Passeig Marítim del Bogatell, Poblenou; ///hears.lure.moguls

Yes, Raval is the city's skateboarding centre but those preferring to practise their tricks and flips without an audience make a beeline for this dedicated skatepark. Not only is the park's giant bowl and wave ramp more chilled but the setting is more scenic.

UNGRAVITY SUP & SURF

Map 5; Carrer de Sevilla 78, Barceloneta; ///exams.rational.renders; www.ungravityboard.com

Anyone expecting an epic surf session will leave Barna disappointed – the Med doesn't always deliver the best waves. The city is the perfect place, however, for first-timers, especially on Barceloneta beach, where the good folk of Ungravity SUP & Surf offer surf lessons. Prefer to try your hand at something a little less exhausting? Ungravity also runs stand-up paddleboarding sessions.

Parks and Picnic Spots

The Mediterranean sun lures locals out to Barna's (surprisingly few) parks and gardens. This is what life here is all about: lazy afternoons and picturesque settings, ideally with a few treats to nibble on.

PARC DEL LABERINT D'HORTA

Map 6; entrance via Passeig dels Castanyers, Horta; ///rich.relaxing.wants
Cascading waterfalls, stone-cut balustrades, a garden maze; this place is, in a word, magical. It's the domain of loved-up couples, giggling their way around the maze; oh, and the odd wild boar that's known to get lost here. The couple of euros to get in is worth it but, if money's tight, come on Wednesdays or Sundays when entry is free.

PARC DE LA CIUTADELLA

Map 5; entrance via Passeig de Pujades, Born; ///tuned.snippet.twigs
Looking for the heart of local life? You've found it. Ciutadella is the people's park and, boy, are the locals fond of it. Families hotfoot it to the boating lake, couples hitch up shaded hammocks, buskers bang on bongos and friends have a kickabout.

JARDINS DE LARIBAL & TEATRE GREC

Map 3; entrance via Passeig de Santa Madrona, Montjuïc;
///composed.lookout.nurture

The labyrinthine Jardins de Laribal is the park of choice for some romantic escapism. Dreamy-eyed locals meander under the park's wisteria-heavy pergola, past the trickling fountains before sketching the fairy-tale-like landscape from the park's steps.

» Don't leave without visiting the amphitheatre, which looks ancient but, like the gardens, was built for the 1929 International Exhibition.

MUHBA TURÓ DE LA ROVIRA

Map 6; entrance via Carrer de Marià Labèrnia, El Carmel;
///grace.geology.pickles

Known to locals as the "bunkers", this site was used by the Republican army during the Civil War. Choosing this specific spot was clearly a no-brainer: the views across the city and out to sea are second to none. Perch yourself atop the bunkers to take it all in – just remember to be mindful and take any litter with you.

JARDÍ BOTÀNIC HISTÒRIC

Map 3; entrance via Avinguda dels Montanyans, Montjuïc;
///slides.jigsaw.leap; www.museuciencies.cat

We know, Barna can be uncomfortable in summer. That's why a lot of locals schlep to this old quarry, which was given back to nature in the 1930s. Home to waterfalls, ponds and the city's tallest trees, the park guarantees cooler climes. Top tip: bug repellent is a must.

JARDINS DE JOAN MARAGALL

Map 3; entrance via Avinguda dels Montanyans, Montjuïc;
///veal.stacks.barmaid

Not many realise there's a royal palace with a perfectly manicured garden hidden on Montjuïc. Dotted with classical-style sculptures and grand water features, Jardins de Joan Maragall is open for just a few hours at weekends. The silver lining? Savvy souls have the place to themselves, save for a few newly engaged couples on photoshoots.

ANELLA OLÍMPICA

Map 3; entrance via Avinguda de l'Estadi, Montjuïc;
///nimbly.clean.defender

On the prowl for a picnic spot with a difference? Look no further than the retro-futurist park where all the Olympic magic went down. Wander through the Olympic park before setting up camp under Santiago Calatrava's bright-white communications tower.

» Don't leave without getting your fill of Olympic trivia at the Museum of Olympics & Sport *(p119)*.

JARDINS DE MOSSÈN COSTA I LLOBERA

Map 3; entrance via Carretera de Miramar, Montjuïc;
///part.unlucky.browser

The green space that launched a thousand Instagram posts, Barna's cactus and succulent garden is a favourite with certain 20-somethings perfecting their social feeds. Stuffed-full of spiky desert plants and swaying palm trees, the garden also has some dreamy sea views.

Liked by the locals

"Montjuïc is my go-to when I need to get away from the city. It's got everything you need: the Olympic park for sunset, gorgeous gardens, big parks for birthday picnics and plenty of space to stretch your legs on a mini hike with sea views."

ALMUDENA LOZA,
PRODUCER AT PROFESSOR FILM

Nearby Getaways

Barcelonans adore their city but when the mercury rises and tourists trickle in, a change of scene is the perfect antidote. Luckily, Barna has various tempting day trips right on its doorstep.

SANT CUGAT DEL VALLÈS

30-minute train from Plaça de Catalunya station; www.santcugat.cat

Just over the mountains from Barna lies the sleepy medieval town of Sant Cugat. Locals make their way to the town's craft and vintage haven of Mercantic, ideally at the weekend when things rev up with live music and food trucks. Rummaging through the warehouses' nooks and crannies, hunting for treasure, a drink in hand – life could be worse.

GIRONA

45-minute train from Sants station; www.girona.cat

Game of Thrones fans will recognize Girona as the Free City of Braavos; gourmands, on the other hand, think of it as the crème de la crème of the foodie world (local restaurant Can Roca has twice been listed as the best in the world). And Barcelonans? It's the perfect weekend getaway, that's what. Sitting at the foot of the Pyrenees, the medieval gem is laced with cobbled streets, ancient balconies and a truly enchanting Jewish quarter. Looking to wow someone? A partner? Your parents? Girona won't let you down.

» Don't leave without devouring an ice cream, decorated with things like burned meringue and flaked almonds, from Rocambolesc Gelateria.

TARRAGONA

1.5-hour train from Sants station; www.tarragonaturisme.cat

Sure, Rome is impressive but Tarragona is spectacular. Founded by the Phoenicians, the city was the Roman capital of the Iberian Peninsula. The result? Historic sites left, right and centre, including an amphitheatre perched right by the sea. But Tarragona is so much more than a relic. Glorious beaches, cosy bars and the Santa Tecla festival, when the streets are packed with *castells* (human towers), keep the city fresh.

SANT POL DE MAR

50-minute bus from Estació del Nord bus station; www.santpol.cat

Ask any local where to head for a chilled beach getaway and they'll say Sant Pol de Mar. This hilly fishing village is pure charm, with its cobbled lanes, *Modernista* buildings and blue waters. Better still, the sandy coves of Roca Grossa are a mere 2 km (1 mile) away – perfect for a secluded skinny dip before an evening feast.

» **Don't leave without** having dinner at La Casa Nostra, a Sicilian restaurant set in a gorgeous 19th-century house by the beach.

EL PENEDÈS

45-minute train from Sants station; www.penedesturisme.cat

Cava gets a bad rap, living in the shadow of its Champagne and Prosecco cousins, but Catalans remain loyal to the sparkling wine produced on their patch. City slickers embark on day trips down to Vilafranca or Sant Sadurní d'Anoia in the Penedès region, where cava hails from. Join them as they hike through the verdant countryside and vineyards, rounding off their walk with an obligatory bottle of bubbly.

Try it!
CYCLING WINE TOUR

Want to really earn that glass of cava? Take a self-guided cycling wine tour with Penedès Ecotours. You'll learn all about the wineries of Vilafranca and the art of cava-making *(www.penedesecotours.com)*.

SITGES

40-minute train from Sants station; www.visitsitges.com

It's a classic with locals and visitors alike. So, no, you might not be alone as you zip down the coast to Sitges. Barcelonans looking to make merry after a long week at work can't resist the town's waterfront restaurants, crafty boutiques and welcoming queer bars. Prefer to while away your stay on the pristine beaches? Expect company in the form of fragile good-timers having an alfresco siesta.

FIGUERES

1.5-hour train from Sants or Passeig de Gràcia stations; www.figueres.cat

It's all about one man, and one man only, in the town of Figueres: local boy Salvador Dalí. Admirers of the surrealist artist call in at the Dalí Theatre-Museum, a wacky red castle crowned with giant eggs (of all things), which houses over-the-top, experiential exhibitions. Truly devout fans pay their respects at the crypt, where the artist lays at rest.

MONTSERRAT

1-hour train from Plaça Espanya station; www.montserratvisita.com

There are two types of pilgrim at Montserrat: Catalan *abuelas* and thrill-seeking mountaineers. The former queue up to kiss "La Moreneta", a sacred statue of the Virgin Mary held in the Benedictine monastery that clings to the Montserrat mountains. No queuing for the climbers; they're busy clambering up the striking mountain face, motivated by the view (and picnic) that awaits at the summit.

Parc de Collserola

Enjoy the views from
TEMPLE EXPIATORI DEL SAGRAT COR

Circle the striking 20th-century church and take in the incredible views. Got the afternoon to kill? Pop to the amusement park next door for thrills and spills.

In 1957, Walt Disney offered to buy **Tibidabo Amusement Park** *for whatever price was named. The park refused.*

3

TIBIDABO

Norman Foster's **Torre de Collserola** *communications tower was built for the 1992 Olympics and became an emblem of the city.*

VALLVIDRERA

Built in 1904, the **Observatori Fabra** *is the world's fourth-oldest functioning observatory. Asteroids and comets are studied here.*

4

Sate your hunger at
CAN MARTÍ

Peckish? Stop for a well-earned lunch at Can Martí. The homely restaurant plates up Mediterranean fare along with more fabulous views.

CARRER DEL BOSC

5

RONDA DE DALT

Head back down to
PEU DEL FUNICULAR

Stroll downhill to Peu de Funicular where the *ferrocarril* train will take you on a short ride back into town.

BONANOVA

0 metres 500
0 yards 500

VIA AUGUSTA

SARRIÀ

PASSEIG DE LA BONANOVA

A morning's hike on
Mount Tibidabo

Tibidabo takes its name from the Latin phrase, *tibi dabo*, or "I will give to you". Legend has it that the devil said these words to Jesus atop this hill, the highest of the Collserolas at 512 m (1,640 ft), as he gestured to the kingdom below. Tibidabo has long provided an escape from the city; an amusement park was built here in the early 20th century, and the hill's inclines are popular with hikers. Join them on the path for a couple of hours' walk.

1. Cafès Gener
Passeig de Sant Gervasi, 59, Sarrià-Sant Gervasi;
www.cafesgener.com
///offers.even.goggles

2. Avinguda del Tibidabo
///rises.chickens.replied

3. Temple Expiatori del Sagrat Cor
Carretera de Vallvidrera al Tibidabo, Tibidabo;
934 17 56 86
///purest.shade.subject

4. Can Martí
Passatge de la Font del Mont, 4, Tibidabo;
www.noucanmarti.com
///partner.puzzles.physical

5. Peu del Funicular
///forced.assorted.securing

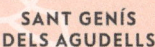 **Observatori Fabra**
///talents.unfair.napped

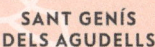 **Tibidabo Amusement Park**
///target.referral.mile

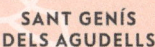 **Torre de Collserola**
///priced.think.emperor

SANT GENÍS
DELS AGUDELLS

RONDA DE DALT

ELS PENITENTS

**Walk along
AVINGUDA DEL TIBIDABO**
Start your ascent on this leafy avenue; you'll pass pretty mansions as you climb up Tibidabo.

2

1

**Grab coffee at
CAFÈS GENER**
Caffeine is essential today. Stop in at Cafès Gener for a coffee to-go.

RONDA DEL GENERAL MITRE

With a little research and preparation, this city will feel like a home away from home. Check out these websites to ensure a healthy, safe stay in Barcelona.

Barcelona
DIRECTORY

SAFE SPACES

Barcelona is a diverse and inclusive city but should you ever feel uneasy or crave community there are spaces that cater to different backgrounds, sexualities and genders.

www.acathi.org
A nonprofit association supporting LGBTQ+ migrants and refugees.

www.ajuntament.barcelona.cat/lgtbi
Barcelona's online and in-person LGBTQ+ centre, providing information, advice and direct assistance for those in the community.

www.ccicbcn.com
A cultural centre providing support and information for and about the Muslim community in Barcelona.

www.fundacioibnbattuta.org
A community centre offering social and employment support to migrants.

www.hostelle.com
A stylish and affordable female-only hostel in Horta-Guinardó.

HEALTH

Healthcare in Spain isn't free to all so make sure you have comprehensive insurance; emergency healthcare is covered by the European Health Insurance Card for EU residents and the UK Global Health Insurance Card for those from the UK. If you need medical assistance, there are many pharmacies and hospitals.

www.bcncheckpoint.com
A sexual health centre primarily aimed at gay men and trans women.

**www.catsalut.gencat.cat/ca/
centres-sanitaris**
*A search engine for types of care and
medical centres in Barcelona.*

www.clinicbarcelona.org
*Barcelona's most important university
hospital, caring for sexual assault victims
and emergency patients.*

www.farmaguia.net
*A directory of all the 24-hour
pharmacies in Barcelona.*

www.turoparkmedical.com
*A private medical centre specializing
in care for foreign patients.*

TRAVEL SAFETY ADVICE
Before you travel – and while you're
here – always keep tabs on what's
happening in Spain. Here are some
useful websites to help keep you safe.

www.aemet.es
*Weather forecasts and advisories,
including extreme temperature alerts.*

**www.ajuntament.barcelona.cat/
guardiaurbana**
*The website of the city's municipal police
force (the Guàrdia Urbana), providing
assistance in the case of an incident.*

www.exteriores.gob.es
*The latest requirements for travelling
to Spain, along with information on
security, health and local regulations.*

www.mossos.gencat.cat
*Online crime reporting for Catalunya's
police force (Mossos d'Esquadra), plus a
list of police stations in the city.*

ACCESSIBILITY
Barcelona is always improving when it
comes to accessibility, but some of its
winding medieval streets and old
infrastructure can prove tricky for
wheelchair users. Here are some
useful websites and resources.

www.barcelona-access.com
*Barcelona's official page for accessible
tourism, listing hotels, cultural sights,
activities and specialist agencies suitable
for those with accessibility needs.*

**www.tmb.cat/en/barcelona/
accessibility-mobility-reduced**
*A list of metro stops specifying ease
of accessibility.*

**www.turismeperatothom.
catalunya.com**
*A resource of sights and activities with
good accessibility across Catalunya.*

INDEX

ACKNOWLEDGMENTS

Meet the illustrator

Award-winning British illustrator David Doran is based in a studio by the sea in Falmouth, Cornwall. When not drawing and designing, David tries to make the most of the beautiful area in which he's based; sea-swimming all year round, running the coastal paths and generally spending as much time outside as possible.

With thanks

DK Travel would like to thank the following people for their contribution to the first edition of this book: Elspeth Beidas, Harri Davies, Tania Gomes, Teresa Gottein Martínez, Ben Hinks, Jordan Lambley, Casper Morris, Lucy Richards, Sofía Robledo and Sam Zucker.

MIX
Paper | Supporting responsible forestry
FSC
www.fsc.org
FSC™ C018179

This book was made with Forest Stewardship Council™ certified paper – one small step in DK's commitment to a sustainable future. Learn more at **www.dk.com/uk/information/sustainability**

A NOTE FROM DK TRAVEL

The world is fast-changing and it's keeping us folk at DK Travel on our toes. We've worked hard to ensure that this edition of Barcelona Like a Local is up-to-date and reflects today's favourite places but we know that standards shift, venues close and new ones pop up in their place. So, if you notice something has closed, we've got something wrong or left something out, we want to hear about it. Drop us a line at travelguides@dk.com

DK | Penguin Random House

THIS EDITION UPDATED BY
Contributor Thom Lampon-Masters
Senior Editor Zoë Rutland
Project Editor Tijana Todorinović
Project Art Editor Ankita Sharma
Cartography Manager Suresh Kumar
Cartographer Ashif
Jacket Designer Laura O'Brien
Jacket Illustrator David Doran
Senior Production Controller Samantha Cross
Managing Art Editor Gemma Doyle
Senior Managing Art Editor Priyanka Thakur
Editorial Director Hollie Teague
Art Director Maxine Pedliham
Publishing Director Georgina Dee

First edition 2022
Published in Great Britain by Dorling Kindersley Limited,
20 Vauxhall Bridge Road, London SW1V 2SA
The authorised representative in the EEA is
Dorling Kindersley Verlag GmbH. Arnulfstr.
124, 80636 Munich, Germany
Published in the United States by DK Publishing,
1745 Broadway, 20th Floor, New York, NY 10019, USA
Copyright © 2022, 2025 Dorling Kindersley Limited
A Penguin Random House Company
24 25 26 27 10 9 8 7 6 5 4 3 2 1
All rights reserved.

A CIP catalog record for this book is available from the British Library.
A catalog record for this book is available from the Library of Congress.
ISSN: 1542 1554
ISBN: 9780 2417 2658 7
Printed and bound in China.
www.dk.com